The Divine Liturgy

Insights into its Mystery

JEAN HANI

The
Divine Liturgy

Insights into its Mystery

ANGELICO PRESS
SOPHIA PERENNIS

Originally published in French as
La Divine Liturgie, Aperçus sur la Messe
© Guy Trédaniel, Éditions de la Maisnie, 1981
First published in USA
by Sophia Perennis © 2008
Angelico Press / Sophia Perennis edition © 2016

Translated by Robert Proctor
Edited by G. John Champoux and Marie Hansen
Series editor: James R. Wetmore

For information, address:
Angelico Press
4709 Briar Knoll Dr.
Kettering, OH 45429
angelicopress.com

Library of Congress Cataloging-in-Publication Data

Hani, Jean.
[Divine liturgie. English]
The divine liturgy: insights into its mystery /
Jean Hani. —1st English ed.

p. cm.
ISBN 978-1-59731-075-8 (pbk: alk. paper)
1. Mass. 2. Catholic Church—Liturgy.
3. Eastern churches—Liturgy. I. Title.
BX2230.3.H3613 2008
264'.02036—dc22   20080003156

Cover Design: Michael Schrauzer

CONTENTS

In memory of
the great liturgist
Mgr. G. Khoury-Sarkis
Chorbishop of the Syrian
Catholic Church
of Antioch

In rendering citations from the Bible, the Tridentine Mass, and the Liturgy of St John Chrysostom into English, the following have been referenced, respectively: *The Authorized Version*; *My Sunday Missal* (J. Stedman [Brooklyn, NY: Confraternity of the Precious Blood, 1938]); and *The Divine Liturgy Explained* (N. M. Elias, [Athens: Astir Publishers, 1979]). The *Anaphora* of St Basil the Great comes from the text of St Andrew's Monastery, Birmingham, U.K.

Introduction

AMONG Eastern Christians it is customary for even laity with an interest in theology and the liturgy to write a commentary on the Mass when they so wish. Two such works written by laymen are famous: *A Commentary on the Divine Liturgy* by Nicholas Cabasilas, sometimes wrongly considered a cleric, and a book of more modest dimensions by the famous Russian writer Nikolai Gogol. Faithful to this tradition, we have undertaken the present work to show our respect for and attachment to the sacrament at the center and heart of the Church's entire life. The western Christian is certainly convinced of this fundamental role of the Mass. However, the at once rational and juridical conception of post-Tridentine and baroque Catholicism, a conception still prevalent today in which the liturgy is bogged down with and practically consumed by private devotions, has for the most part rid him of the desire to fathom the extraordinary depths of the mystery celebrated at the altar, preventing him from grasping the fullness of its beauty. The Mass is, in fact, a masterpiece of beauty, for it is a manifestation of Divinity, one of whose primary attributes is Beauty. The liturgy's beauty has, however, struck certain artists, like Claudel who wrote after a celebration at Notre Dame: 'It consisted of the profoundest and grandest poetry, and the most august gestures that have ever been confided to human beings. I cannot have enough of the spectacle of the Mass.'[1]

---

1. *Contacts et circonstance*, 1938. Cf. M. Proust in a *Chronique* of 16 August, 1914: 'The preservation of the greatest conceivable artistic collection, which one would spare no expense in reconstituting if it were to cease to exist, to wit the Mass in the cathedrals, makes it the duty of the government to assist the Catholic Church in the maintenance of a cult which contributes more to the preservation of the noblest French art than [other] societies having an arguable artistic goal....' Poor Proust, if he were to return today! ...

Another factor hiding the depth and beauty of the Mass from the faithful is perhaps the word itself which, it needs to be said, was very poorly chosen. *Mass* comes from the Latin *missa*, the past participle of *mittere*, meaning, 'to send'. In their official ceremonial the Romans, in order to dismiss assemblies, used the formula *missa est contio*, which is equivalent to 'the meeting is adjourned'. This formula was used by the Christian liturgy at Rome, whence the *Ite missa est*, to which *contio* should be added: 'Go, the meeting is adjourned.' This was, then, simply a formula of dismissal. Later, towards the fifth century, the word *missa* became a noun, and in Christian terminology gradually designated the assembly gathered for the Holy Sacrifice, and finally the Holy Sacrifice itself. But the word neither 'speaks' to the spirit, nor orients it towards the content of the sacrifice. The eastern Churches use words that all, in one way or another, relate to the idea of holiness or the sacred. The Copts use the Greek word *hagiasmos*, 'consecration', to designate the Mass. The Ethiopians call it *qeddas* from a Semitic root meaning 'holy' (in Arabic 'Mass' is called *quddas*). The Syrian Churches say *qurobho*, an Aramaic word meaning, 'approach', 'access', thus referring to the role of the Holy Sacrifice, which is to provide access to the altar, to draw us closer to God. The same root in Arabic gives the word *taqarrab*, which means, 'to approach the holy table', 'to communicate'. Finally, the churches of the Greek rite use the well-known expression *Divine Liturgy*, which has the sense, more or less, of 'divine service'. One sees that all these words have the advantage of placing the accent on the depth and sacredness of the Holy Mysteries.

If in the first place our book is intended to be a personal homage to this Divine Liturgy, it also has another purpose. Without any doubt, the gravest symptom in the crisis the Western Church is currently undergoing—its repercussions on art were already denounced in our book *The Symbolism of the Christian Temple*—is the calling in question of the very meaning and content of the Mass, given, as stated above, that it is the heart and vital center of the Church, and we deem it proper to come to its defence. Our intention, though, is not to become involved in recent theological quarrels on this issue. In this study our point of view is neither that of the theologian nor the liturgist. Most assuredly, we have consulted and studied the essential writings on the theology and liturgy of the Mass, and if, in the pages that follow, we refrain from citing any such authors, this is solely to avoid rekindling these quarrels at a time when tempers are sufficiently roused for the simple mention of a name to whip up passions in the opposing camp. But, to put the reader's mind at rest, we have done everything necessary to say only what is perfectly orthodox. If we have made some mistakes, may God pardon us.

Our point of view, then, is neither that of a theologian nor liturgist, but a historian of religions. What we wish to show is that the Christian Mass is illumined by studies concerning the universal patterns of the sacred to which it conforms. Most assuredly, Christian worship has its specificity, but that is for the theologian and liturgist to spell out. What we propose to do is unravel the features in Christian worship linking it to the universality of the sacred.[2]

Without doubt the history of religions, with the aid of anthropology, ethnology, and linguistics has brought something irreplaceable to the understanding of Christianity and we should not despise the acquisitions of these sciences. Let us be quite clear: in our previous works we have criticized, even seemed to reject modern sciences. However, such an attitude would be surprising on our part; we who have spent the greater part of our life doing research in the domain of classical philology and the history of religions, and teaching these sciences to students. On the contrary, we think one should fearlessly use the results of these sciences in explaining Christianity. At the same time, what we reject is the 'spirit', or 'philosophy' if one prefers, that animates these sciences among a majority of our contemporaries, and vitiates at its roots their line of development and their conclusions, without however impairing the objective value of the documentary material gathered. The 'spirit' here is that of the supposed principle of science's autonomy with respect to religious truth and metaphysics; much is made of this, even among ecclesiastics. And this is one reason why it is urgent to look at things in a different 'spirit'. For some years, in fact, a certain number of books

---

2. This proposal has already been outlined in our book on the temple, which has led us, understandably and pardonably, we hope, to take up again here a certain number of ideas 'already treated there'. This remark refers to the present Chapter 4.

have appeared, written by ecclesiastics or persons connected with ecclesiastical milieux, which also propose to use the history of religions, anthropology, ethnology, and linguistics to elucidate the facts of Christian religion and worship. Unhappily the authors of these studies, who for the most part depend on the dominant ideology of our universities, have come to support very questionable theses that end up diluting the substance of religions. The real results obtained, principally by the history of religions, using modern research methods, need to be restudied in a different light and integrated into a superior perspective which governs its use. As for us, we use these findings by subjecting them on the one hand to theology, and on the other to metaphysics and the universal sacred Tradition.

The principal contribution of these human sciences to the understanding of the liturgy concerns the role of rite and symbol.

One reason for the above mentioned 'bogging down' of the liturgy is, in fact, the sterilization of the imaginative side through the intellectualism and desiccating rationalism rife since the seventeenth century. Regarding this, it is impossible to exaggerate the damage of later Aristotelianism and above all Descartes. Gradually, under the influence of this cast of mind, Christians ended up no longer understanding the rites and great symbols that are the very flesh of the liturgy, which, as a result, was reduced to an official cult without impact upon the faithful. Now these symbols, which animate the rites, are essential to the life of the liturgy, and the importance of both symbols and rites is increasingly recognized today by the human sciences. Some years ago we read the following lines in a Paris newspaper, which would certainly not have been found there one or two generations earlier:

> Rites are the ensemble of attitudes and actions making for a recognition of, participation in, and benefiting from the supernatural.... Man is extremely demanding with regard to rites. The more the daily world changes, the more he attaches himself to the permanence of the rite. Every change in the rites provokes surprise, irritation, nay incomprehension, criticism and disaffection. Contrary to the conclusions of a superficial reasoning, one could also very probably say that *rites outlast beliefs whereas*

beliefs do not outlast rites. It is in any case a grave error to think that rites can degenerate into anarchy without beliefs doing the same.[3]

Also noticeable almost everywhere these days is opposition regarding symbolism on the part of clerics and their followers, all under the influence of the much-celebrated Bultmann who on this point relayed the Cartesian influence while aggravating it. Bultmann rejected symbolism and myth as inadequate to both the modern scientific spirit and the gospel message, and the clerics, divorced from tradition and wishing to appear 'emancipated', rushed all the more eagerly into Bultmannism. And they did so without in the least taking into account that this thesis, the offshoot of the religious philosophy sprung from the 'Age of Enlightenment', was shown completely out of date ever since studies in the history of religions, anthropology, ethnology, and also depth psychology, battling in the breach the rationalistic point of view on myth and symbolism, had each in its own way restored to the latter all their value. These studies showed that we are dealing here with a mode of thinking absolutely basic to man and inscribed even in his corporeal being. The sciences in question have shown the irreplaceable character of the symbol, which expresses a reality transmissible in no other way. Let us call it the specific vector of the sacred: by this means Christian salvation penetrates to the very depths of the soul. Religious representations, such as those produced in the West since the seventeenth century, that reject these symbols or allow them to fall into escheat, or reduce their ritual to a schematic unfolding, lose their efficacy. Sacred symbols, in fact, are connected to the constitutive archetypal images of the human soul; through them the soul, in its state of union with the body, receives the sacred message of the cosmos, which, itself, is for this being the intermediary whereby the divine touches and penetrates it.

Most assuredly, we have no need to appeal to the human sciences to justify symbolism, which the great sacred, universal and eternal Tradition, of supra-human essence, does sufficiently. But, after all, it

---

3. G. Fourastié in *Le Figaro*, June 7, 1973

is not bad to know that the profane point-of-view itself, through it own methods, tends to rejoin a part of the transcendent truth.

Considerable help in understanding the symbolism of the rites of the Mass is provided by the liturgies of the Oriental Churches, liturgies that are far more stable than those of the West and rich in poetry. This leads us to say a word about the manner in which we have conducted our study, a study dealing principally with the Roman Mass for an easily understandable reason.[4] We shall, however, constantly appeal to the Greek, Syrian, Maronite, Armenian, Coptic, and Ethiopian Churches' texts of the Mass, in order to shed light upon the different aspects of the eucharistic celebration, which in its essential depth is without doubt one in all apostolic churches, but, in other respects, very different in its modes of expression. This will also be an opportunity to make known these liturgies, so ignored in the West, and to pay homage, very modestly, to our venerable eastern Christianities, the oldest, going back to the Apostolic age, Christianities too often martyred in the course of history, and even today, tragically, by the total official indifference of the great nations and nearly total indifference of western Christians.

---

4. We follow the text of the old Roman ritual. For some years, in fact, the Latin Church has used a new ritual from which, curiously, certain characteristic traits of the sacred and, in particular, of the category of the sacrifice are missing, which noticeably differentiates this ritual from those of all other Apostolic Churches. This new ritual also appears deficient in the eyes of the historian of religions.

1

The Sacrifice

THE MASS, or divine liturgy, is essentially a sacrifice, as proclaimed by one of the names frequently given it: the Holy Sacrifice. It is not, as some would have it, a simple sacrifice of praise, nor a simple meal of remembrance, nor even solely the commemoration of a sacrifice accomplished at another time. Memorial of a violent and bloody sacrifice, that of Golgotha, it is itself a true sacrifice, the same as that of Golgotha, endowed, therefore, with a power of reconciliation and propitiation.[1] Without a doubt the Mass has a much greater scope and encompasses other supernatural realities than this bloody sacrifice, just as, moreover, the notion of sacrifice possesses a far wider acceptation than that of the bloody immolation of a victim. We shall have many occasions to speak of this again. This notion of immolation nevertheless remains capital, as much in the theology of the redemption as in the Mass, which is its ritual perpetuation. It is therefore from this central reality of the Mass, which is like its kernel, that one needs to start in order to understand the eucharistic celebration.

The sacrifice of Christ, like the whole of His mission, was accomplished in continuance of the Jewish tradition of the Old Testament. We shall therefore start by taking a look at the different forms of sacrifice in the old Law, which will lead us to conclude that the Cross of Christ recapitulates the preceding sacrifices while tran-

---

1. Council of Trent, Sess. 22, Can.1 (Denziger-Umberg, n. 948): '*Si quis dixerit in missa non offerri Deo verum et proprium sacrificium aut quod offerri non sit aliud quam nobis Christum ad manducandum dari, anathema sit*'; Can. 3. (ibid., n. 950): '*Si quis dixerit missae sacrificium tantum esse laudis et gratiarum actionis aut nudam commemorationem sacrificii in cruce peracti, non autem propitiatorium, etc.*'

scending them, and yet, to a certain extent, receives its explanation from them. Having thus reinserted the sacrifice of Calvary within its ethno-religious context, so to say, we shall subsequently be able to address more profitably the analysis of the sacrifice itself, from first the phenomenological then the metaphysical point of view.

The Hebrews knew and practised numerous types of sacrifice. Besides the offering of incense, which constituted a sacrifice and about which we shall say more later, there was first of all a bloodless sacrifice called *minha*, 'oblation', whose origin was an offering of the first fruits of the earth. In the *minha* one offered flat cakes made of flour, oil and incense, some of which were burnt, that is to say consecrated, while the priests consumed the rest. The best known form of the *minha* is the rite of the 'shewbread' (*lehem panim*), consisting of twelve loaves, representing the twelve tribes of Israel; they were placed on a golden table in the Temple, and above each a little incense was burnt. Every Sabbath fresh loaves were put out and those of the previous week were given to the priests.

Among the blood sacrifices, the most important was the holocaust, the transcendent element of the cult, called *olah* in Hebrew.[2] The Greek word *holocauste* means, 'entirely burnt'. In effect, the victim, generally a bull or young bullock, after being bled to death, was totally consumed by the fire on the altar, which signified that it was entirely consecrated and offered to God. The Hebrew word comes from the verb *alah*, which means to 'ascend', alluding to the smoke rising towards heaven, which is to say, symbolically towards the heavenly abode of God. The blood of the victim was scattered at the four corners of the altar. This rite had great significance, for blood, in effect, corresponds to the transcendent essence of man, which is seated in the heart. Now the slain animal was substituted for a man, this being marked by the preliminary rite of the *semikha*, in which the offerer placed his hand on the head of the victim and presented it at the altar. The flow of blood from the victim signified that the offerer re-attached and offered himself to God through the altar and symbolically followed the itinerary of the animal whose flesh, sublimated by the fire, 'ascended' to God.

---

2. Lev. 9:17, Num. 28:34, Exod. 29:42, Ezek. 46:13, 15; 29:39, Esd. 3:5.

The *zebah shelamim*, or 'sacrifice of peace', that was performed at great solemnities,[3] was a sacrifice of *communion* with God. A part of the immolated victim, the blood and fat, was burnt and thereby offered to God, while the rest served as food for the faithful and the priests at a sacred *banquet*. There were three types of *zebah shelamim*, the most interesting for us being the *zebah todah*, that is the 'sacrifice of praise' or 'thanksgiving', because these labels have been and still are applied to the Mass; it is also called *Eucharist*, that is 'thanksgiving', and, in several places in the ritual's text, is designated in Latin by the expression *sacrificium laudis*. The Hebrew rite started with a chant of thanksgiving followed by the immolation of the victim, during which a circumambulation of the altar was made. Loaves and libations of wine were also offered, especially a cup called 'the cup of salvation', an expression taken from Psalm 116, one of the Hallel Psalms,[4] which is also to be found in the Roman Mass: at the moment of his communion, the priest says 'What shall I render unto the Lord for all his benefits toward me? I will take the cup of salvation and call upon the Name of the Lord.'[5]

The *hattat* sacrifice was a rite of purification and expiation for sin; there too the offerer placed his hands upon the victim (young bullock, he- or she-goat, ewe, two pigeons or doves) a part of which was burnt and the rest consumed by the priests. Attached to this rite was the important annual ceremony called the Feast of Expiation or the Great Pardon (*yom kippur*) the purpose of which was to purify

---

3. Exod. 23:18, 34:25.

4. Psalms 112–117.

5. The unfolding of this Hebrew sacrifice closely resembles the sacrifice most often performed in ancient Greece, the *thysia*, which followed nearly the same ritual pattern, with the dividing of the victim between the divinity and the faithful, hymns, and a banquet (above all in the celebration of the Mysteries; cf. *Sylloge Inscript. Graec.*, 736). This sacrifice was called *charistirion* and *eucharistirion*, which means: 'Sacrifice of Thanksgiving'. It is quite obvious that we need not conclude from this, as many have felt compelled to, that the Christian sacrifice was based on the *thysia*. Christianity we shall see had no need to be inspired by the Greeks: it sufficed for it to draw, as did Jesus, from the Jewish tradition. If the Greek *thysia* resembled the *zebah shelamim*, it is quite simply because the religious era under consideration followed, in the different religions, the same sacrificial rule inherited from the sacred Tradition adapted to that moment of history.

the priest and all the people from the sins of the year. It was celebrated on the tenth of the month of Tisri in the following way: the High Priest first offered a young bull and ram for his sins and those of the whole priesthood through placing his hands on the animals' heads and confessing his sins. He then offered two he-goats and a ram for the sins of the people. After censing the sanctuary, he immolated the bull and sprinkled the former with the blood of the victim; he then sacrificed one of the two he-goats, and with its blood sprinkled the sanctuary again, then the court, and anointed the altar of holocausts. The second he-goat was the object of a particular and well-known rite: the High Priest with his hands extended over it, confessed his and the people's sins thereby loading the animal with them. He then attached a long scarlet ribbon to its head, because among the Jews scarlet was the symbolic color of sin,[6] after which a man led it to a deserted place from where he hurled it down from a high cliff. Thus the animal 'took away' the sins of Israel, whence the name 'scapegoat'.

If we have dwelt somewhat on the Feast of Expiation, this is because it assumes a certain importance for understanding the meaning and importance of Christ's sacrifice. The latter, we have said, integrates all the earlier sacrificial rites. This is particularly so concerning the rite of *yom kippur*, as St Paul has shown. In the *Epistle to the Hebrews* he compared Christ to the High Priest who once a year enters the Holy of Holies alone,

> not without blood, which he offered for himself, and for the errors of the people.... But Christ being come an high priest of good things to come, by a greater and more perfect tabernacle, not made with hands, that is to say, not of this building; neither by the blood of goats and calves, but by his own blood he entered in once into the holy place, having obtained eternal redemption for us. For if the blood of bulls and of goats, and the ashes of an

6. Cf. Isa. 1:18. Likewise among the Egyptians red also symbolized evil. Cf. J. Hani, *La religion egyptienne dans la pensée de Plutarch*, Paris, 1976, p272 ff., 446, where we again see that the Egyptians undoubtedly practised a comparable rite to that of the scapegoat. Similar rites are encountered elsewhere. In Greece, it was even performed over men, called *pharmakoi* (op. cit., p278 with references).

heifer sprinkling the unclean, sanctifieth to the purifying of the flesh: how much more shall the blood of Christ, who through the eternal Spirit offered himself without spot to God, purge your conscience from dead works to serve the living God? (Heb. 9:7–14; cf. ibid., 15–28 and 13:10–14).

The comparison made by St Paul holds for the other forms of Hebraic sacrifice. This is obvious for the holocaust: the sacrifice of Christ is the absolute holocaust; the offerings of the first fruits and the *zebah shelamim* already outline the pattern of the Mass. But it is above all the sacrifice of the Passover, the sacrifice of the Pascal lamb and the meal that follows, that should engage our attention, for it is this type of sacrifice that Christ, after transforming it, chose to make the sacrifice of the New Testament. We shall need to study closely the integration of the Jewish Passover in the unfolding of the Divine Liturgy. Let it suffice for the moment to recall its essential points.

The Jewish Passover belongs to the sort of sacrifice in which the animal victim that has been offered is entirely eaten by men in the name of the Divinity. It is a sacrifice of communion, like the *zebah shelamim*. The officiant was the head of the family, and also the priest, for the sacrifice of the Passover was also offered at the Temple. This rite was of great importance to the Jews since it commemorated, as we know, the liberation from slavery in Egypt and the entry into the Promised Land.[7] The Passover, or *pesach* in Hebrew, meaning 'passage', the passage from exile into the Promised Land, was the symbol that Christ had only to 'vitalize' in some way, in order to make it the efficacious sign of the passage from death to life, from the shadows to the light; such that through the sacrificed Divine Lamb, we are transferred to the Kingdom of the Father.

Sacrifice is regarded as so universal and as practised by all peoples throughout all ages that it is generally taken for an unquestionable, self-evident fact. We know and admit quite naturally that it is

---

7. Exod. 12:25 and 27.

necessary for paying homage to God and for the expiation of sin, without troubling to look further. But in reality, when we think about it, the relationship between sacrifice on the one hand and praise and expiation on the other, a relationship that seems self-evident, is not so easy to explain.

To really understand the phenomenon of sacrifice, it is important then to study more closely its nature and meaning. What at bottom is sacrifice? How is it explained? What are its origins, its nature, and scope?

Sacrifices fall into the most general category of sacred rites. Among the latter, we need to distinguish fundamental from auxiliary rites. The first are those which introduce man into the domain of the sacred, such as all rites of admission to a traditional community, for example Christian baptism, the different initiations and funerary rites. The second are prayers and, precisely, rites of offering and sacrificial rites. While called 'auxiliary', this should not hide their importance, or better, their necessity. For rites of admission, for example, only introduce man to the sacred in a virtual manner: he can only effectively assimilate the sacred through those practices making up the prayers and sacrifices that accompany the whole course of his life.

The notion of sacrifice, where the word is purely and simply synonymous with immolation, is much broader than its habitual meaning leads us to understand. As its etymology indicates, it refers in the widest way to the *sacred*; the Latin expression for 'to sacrifice' is *rem divinam facere*, 'to accomplish the divine act'; and the word *sacrificium*, composed of *sacer* and *facere*, has the same sense: 'sacred action'.[8] The verb *sacrificare* means not only 'to sacrifice' but also 'to consecrate'. The term *sacrifice* then refers very accurately to its object, such as mentioned a moment ago, which is to introduce a being into the domain of the sacred. The conjoint notion of immolation came only afterwards.

Sacrifice could be defined as the act with the twin aim of making a gift to God and sanctifying the man who makes it.

---

8. Obviously, the Greek word, *thysia*, originally only evoked the 'smoke' of the sacrifice.

Why a gift to God? It is a gift in return. In fact, life is a gift of the Creator, as is everything, such as the food that serves to maintain this life. And conscious and responsible beings, to spiritually realize the meaning of this gift by referring to its symbolic quality, and, at the same time, to make it more abundant and long-lasting, need to offer the Creator in return a part of what He gives. In this way, certain secondary forms of sacrifice are explained, such as the libations at table practised in ancient Greece or India, or again, the tithe. In the first case, one only ate and drank after offering 'God's share', according to the mediaeval expression. In the second, one gives up a tenth of what one possesses in order to attest, through this gesture, that all that one has one holds from God, and at the same time guarantee the continuance of these blessings by preventing the circle of prosperity from closing.

If one wants to go into the history, or more exactly, pre-history of sacrifice and research its origin, it is important first of all to rid oneself of the veritable pseudo-scientific 'dogmas' proclaimed in the majority of studies in the history of religion or in anthropology. We have read astounding assertions from the pen of an author whose work on sacrifice is among those considered to be very important, his theory being based on the grossest evolutionist presuppositions. But what is graver still is that these assertions are for the most part taken into account without further ado by ecclesiastical authors, some of whom are today renowned theologians. It is truly distressing to see purely profane 'scientific' theories, totally lacking in a solid basis, honored in this way by people who at the same time refuse to take seriously traditional sciences that draw their value from both metaphysical principles and Revelation. Thus, we shall never understand how a Catholic theologian can attempt to trace the origins of sacrifice starting from the evolutionist presupposition and seeing 'primitive' man as 'savage', or even still close to an animal whence he has 'obviously' sprung, and at the same time believe in the account of the first chapters of Genesis, without perceiving the fundamental incompatibility separating the two ways of seeing, in spite of the heady lucubrations and acrobatic capers whereby 'Catholic' evolutionists have tried to reconcile them.

By basing oneself then on the traditional doctrine under its two aspects, metaphysical and religious, one can properly consider the problem of the origin of sacrifice.

In the state of innocence, in the world of Eden, it was not necessary to sacrifice in the sense we intend. Being in no way subjected to matter, man quite naturally made that gift to God which is the obligatory response of the creature to the Creator, an absolutely pure gift, entirely spiritual: the gift of the heart. In a surge of perfect love he surrendered himself and everything created to God. After the fall, things were no longer the same. Man was cast down from the higher spiritual plane onto the physical material plane, his fault, or fall, having consisted precisely in the decision to egoistically appropriate the created in place of surrendering it unreservedly to God.

The consequences of this fall would have been irremediable if the Divine Mercy had not intervened to palliate them. So it was that the Messengers from Heaven—whoever they may have been, this is not the place to discuss them—imparted to man the sacrifice desired and determined by God, as a way of remedying, in part, the consequences of this spiritual catastrophe.

The goal of sacrifice is to restore man to the level from which he fell, to place him again on the spiritual plane. To get there, it is necessary to effect a *transfer*. Let us explain. In a certain way, the only means to redress the fault and its consequences was death, because, precisely, death snatches us from the physical and material world, and, moreover, it is quite clear in Genesis that God decided that man, having become a sinner, would die. He did not, however, need to die immediately; humanity did not need to be annihilated, annihilating at the same time the plane of creation. Man needed to live a certain time outside the paradisal state, in a fallen and materialized state. Sacrifice was the means to operate symbolically and ritually a 'death' to the material world and transfer to the original spiritual world. In a certain way, all sacrifice is fundamentally a human sacrifice, as is shown by the already mentioned rite of the *semikha*, about which we shall speak again soon. To be sure, actual physical human sacrifice is an aberrant and monstrous deviation, found among certain peoples who have degenerated in one way or another: but it is the deviation of an idea, or better, a profound necessity imperfectly understood in a gross manner. In the normally conceived sacrifice, it is by way of an *intermediary* and a *substitution* that man's transfer to the spiritual world is effected. Man is transferred by another physical being, or object, which is substituted for him and which itself is transferred through the rite to the spiritual plane. Its mechanism is as follows. The being or object is *offered* to the divinity and thus becomes sacred through the rite which integrates it into the domain of the sacred; and, at the same time, being identified, through substitution, with the man who offers it, it integrates him into that realm. The being or object sacrificed becomes the *mediator* between the world-below and the one On-High.

We have spoken of the object offered. In fact, it is not only a living creature that can be substituted: it can also be a vegetable, flowers for example, a food, like bread or wine, or even a fabricated object. Thus, for example, in ancient Egypt, the daily ritual required a double offering: one to the Eye of Horus, a solar symbol, and one to Maat. Maat was the entity representing Justice and Truth and, more generally, divine energy.[9] The priest offered up a statuette of Maat in the sanctuary: through the offering of this statuette, the soul of the man rejoined the divinity in the spiritual universe.

But more often it was an animal that was substituted for the man in the sacrifice, the animal being close to man; at least in the case of the higher animals, and it is they that were most often chosen for the sacrifice. The blood sacrifice was the sacrifice par excellence. Now that these sacrifices have ceased nearly everywhere, we find it difficult today to understand why the blood sacrifice was necessary, in particular for the expiation of sin. This, however, is an important question, for the most spectacular expiatory blood sacrifice was, dare we say, that of Christ, but this involves understanding why.

The blood sacrifice is like a voluntary death: through the intermediary of the sacrificed animal, the man voluntarily 'dies' to the phenomenal and material world, and, through this act, is at least virtually restored to the spiritual universe, according to the process described above. Sacralized through the rite of offering, the animal

9. A. Moret, *Rituel du culte journalier*, p148 ff., who points out that the name Maat, the neuter passive participle of maa, means both, 'that which is real, true, just' and 'that which is offered'.

serves in some way to graft man onto divinity. This is why, in certain cases, the offerer put on the skin of the sacrificed animal. By donning it, he was reborn in the form of a supernaturalized being.[10] In light of this custom, St Paul's formula takes on its full meaning and power when he speaks of 'putting on the Lord Jesus Christ' (Rom. 13:14).

We see, then, the necessity for immolation, which refutes the assertions of certain authors who have claimed that the death of an animal, though necessary, was not essential. Others, still in the same vein, have claimed that the sacrifice did not always include immolation, citing the case of the offering of foods, flowers, libations of wine, etc., which according to them reinforces the preceding thesis. But in reality this is not accurate, for it is to forget that the bread is already the result of the immolation, by man, of the wheat, which is threshed, ground and 'burnt' in the cooking. As for the wine, it does not exist without the 'passion', as mentioned, of grapes pressed, triturated, and transformed through fermentation. Besides, they all have to die finally a second time in being eaten after the offering by the divinity, that is to say the priest or offerer. It is no different with the oblation of incense, which is burnt, or the flower. A magnificent flower is cut and dies in order to be offered. It thereby bears witness both to its beauty, which is the reflection of the Divine Beauty, and its nothingness in the face of absolute Beauty; its death in the offering attests the supremacy of the Essence.

To return to the blood sacrifice, we still need to consider something of great importance in explaining this type of oblation. For all or nearly all traditions, blood is like the vehicle of the vital principle, or living soul, which is affirmed in particular by the Bible (Deut. 12:23, Lev. 17:10–11). It is the milieu where the psychic elements bind with the corporeal modality. When one ate the flesh of the victim or drank its blood, one absorbed and assimilated its vital force. But, and this is important, a *consecrated* vital force which, as a result, vehicled the energy of the god. The same consideration also explains the rites of purification and of alliance. We have already

10. For example, in the Dionysian or in the Egyptian rite called *tikenu*; cf. A Moret, *Mystères égyptiens*, Paris, 1923, p 41 ff.

pointed out examples of the first. As for the second, they occupy an important place in the Old Testament. The 'alliance' between God and His people is sealed by a 'pact of blood' (Exod. 24:8; Zech. 9:11). The offered and sacrificed victim, accepted by God, seals the alliance according to the following process. The animal represents the people, it's blood the life of this people; the animal is offered, consecrated and, by that, 'passes' to the divine world where its blood is charged with divine energy. God, then, sends the offering, bearing His blessing, back to the people, the blessing of adoption with all the beneficial consequences of this act. One will realize the full importance of this sacrificial process of alliance when one comes to see that it constitutes, at a higher level, the mechanism of the Christic sacrifice itself, that of the New Covenant.

We alluded above to the rite of eating the offering, which leads us to dwell a little upon ritual meals, the meals of communion, which accompany a good number of types of sacrifice. The meal, or sacred banquet, assumed such importance in the different cults that the majority of modern scholars have wished to see in it the origin of all sacrifices. This is certainly a mistake, which should nevertheless not hide the important role of the sacred banquet.

Its practice was particularly developed in Ancient Greece. Perhaps the most characteristic case was that of the prytanes at Athens. The prytanes, representing the tribes, formed a body charged with organizing the deliberations of the Senate, and enjoyed great prestige. Housed at the Prytaneum or at the Tholos, they would eat there, close to the altar of Hestia, which was the center of the Greek state: from this very fact, the meal assumed a sacred character. The prytanes wore crowns, the sacred symbol worn also by the priests for the sacrifices, and even their persons were considered sacred, at least for the duration of the meal. In fact, the prytanes ate there in the name of the city, and the meal established a connection between the human group and the supernatural universe, concentrated in the hearth of Hestia, which provided the community with *mana*. We know moreover of many other ritual meals at Athens, for example those organized by the tribes on the occasion of the great festivals, like the Dionysiae and the Panathenaea, and that of the women which followed the sacrifice on the third day of the festival of the

Thesmophoriae. The most interesting, however, were the sacred meals held in the *thiases*, the religious confraternities uniting the devotees of a divinity, because this type of religious community was not dissimilar to the original Christian communities which, in Greece and at Rome, were organized somewhat along the same lines and were also practising a similar rite under the name of *agape*. In the thiases, besides the great festivals spread over the year, the cult allowed for a monthly sacrifice followed by a communal meal, which became ever more important as Antiquity drew to a close.

This rite was encountered in the cult of Attis, where Firmicus Maternus practised it. He spoke about it after converting to Christianity and established a parallel between it and the Christian meal.[11] The same applied in the cult of Mithras, where one drank a mixture of bread, water, and the sap of the plant called *haoma*. And, with the cult of Isis and Sarapisin, we see a special hall in the Iseum of Pompey reserved for the meals of the initiates, and curious invitations to this type of banquet have even been found.[12]

As a matter of fact, in the heart of traditional societies the ritual character of the meal even appears in ordinary meals, for the ordinary meal already induces man to raise his thoughts to the Divinity. Here, more than elsewhere perhaps, man appears as the recipient; he has to receive food in order to survive, and he understands that this nourishment *comes* to him from *Another*, to whom then the prayer of thanksgiving rises. 'The eyes of all wait upon thee; and thou givest them their meat in due season. Thou openest thy hand, and satisfiest the desire of every living thing,' says the Psalmist (Psalm 144). This is why in normal societies every meal is in some way a religious rite, the most important action of which was the already mentioned libation to the gods. The Greek meal commenced with a libation to Zeus Sotirios (Saviour) accompanied with a prayer and the ritual wish *agathou daimonos*, 'good luck!' In the ritual meal following a sacrifice, the process of sanctification of

11. F. Maternus, *De errore prof. relig.*, 18, 1.
12. The following is one of them: 'Chaeremon invites you to eat at the table of Lord Sarapis, in the Sarapeon, tomorrow the 15th at the ninth hour.' Cf. *Harvard Theological Review* 41, (1948) 9, 29.

the faithful was invariably the same as the one described above. Food and drink were offered to the divinity and accordingly incorporated into the divine world; in return the share taken by man joined him to the divine world. The food is given to God who lets man share this gift, thereby vivifying and, ultimately, divinizing him through the participation, whence the expression, 'to eat the god'. This last stage was especially known in the Dionysiac cult where the animal sacrificed, generally a fawn, the hypostasis of Dionysius, was immolated and then consumed by the bacchants, this incorporation throwing them into ecstasy. The same occurred with wine, the other hypostasis of Dionysius.[13]

The communal meal was known among the Hebrews and, as already mentioned, furnished Christ with the basis of His sacrament. We shall have to study this in detail, which will then be the occasion to see what a communion meal was in the Old Testament.

But first, in order to conclude this general exposition on the sacrifice, we need to say a word on the significance of the holocaust. In this type of sacrifice, the immolated victim is entirely consumed by fire. Originally it was a transcendent fire, the fire of heaven, which fell upon the altar at the prayer of the officiant, when the latter had the power to make it descend. We see examples of this in the Bible in the case of Noah or the Prophet Elijah. In due course, a ritual fire replaced the celestial fire: still, it was its symbol, and involved a fire that had nevertheless been 'blessed'.

The meaning of the holocaust is obvious. It is the total, absolute, sacrifice. The victim is not shared between the divinity and man: it is given entirely to the divinity. The divine fire, which falls upon it, takes possession of it and the smoke released from it rises to heaven whither the subtle essence of the victim is borne in the direction of the 'heavenly tabernacle'. The holocaust symbolizes and realizes the total gift of the offerer. But it also has a wider meaning, symbolizing and prefiguring the cosmic sacrifice, for, in fact, it is the whole cosmos that needs to be offered and transferred to the divine plane.

Christ's sacrifice and its memorial, the Mass, also, and supereminently so, has this cosmic dimension. Once again, then, we find

---

13. Cf. Euripides, *Bacchantes*, 284.

ourselves recalling the operation whereby Jesus integrated, recapitulated, and fulfilled every type of sacrifice in His unique sacrifice.
But this time we can state precisely the meaning of the operation.
We have seen how St Paul, in the *Epistle to the Hebrews*, identified
Christ with the Hebrew high priest, entering the Holy of Holies at
the Feast of Expiation, to bring His own blood for the remission of
sins. Another fact will allow the parallel to be pushed further and
show how it was even in certain details that the action of Christ was
inscribed in Jewish sacrificial customs. When Pilate handed Jesus,
who had declared himself a king, over to the Roman soldiers, the
latter, to mock him, placed a crown of thorns on his head and a red
or purple cloak on his shoulders. They did so because among the
Romans, as among the majority of the peoples of antiquity, purple
was the color of kings. But, by a coincidence that was not by chance,
this red cloak showed that Jesus had become the 'man of sin', as the
Scripture says. In fact, as we have seen, red was the symbol of evil
and transgression, which is why, as was said above, the high priest
attached a long scarlet ribbon to the scapegoat. Who can fail to see
from this the extraordinary and mysterious interconnection of
signs that constituted this episode with Pilate? Clothed in that
mocking royal purple, Christ appeared to the Jews, not as a mock
king but as Hazazel, the Scapegoat; and perhaps this circumstance
gives a particular resonance to their cry, 'May his blood be upon us!'

From the tribunal of Pilate, Jesus proceeded to Golgotha where
the sacrifice was completed. This then was the holocaust of holocausts, the absolute and transcendent holocaust. Here Christ sacrificed His mortal body, and this sacrifice manifested the integral gift
of self to the Supreme Being, and revealed the existence of the
'Kingdom of God' as the only reality. Here Christ is both the victim
sacrificed and the sacrificer. The victim, the offering, is super-emi-
nently transferred from the terrestrial physical world to the supernatural world; this victim encompasses all victims and all material
offerings, become from now on unnecessary. High priest of His
own sacrifice, Christ 'officiated' on the cross, the cosmic symbol,
planted atop Golgotha, the cosmic mountain, as we shall see in
more detail regarding the liturgical celebration. This is to say that
the sacrifice of Calvary transfers the totality of the spatio-temporal

human cosmos to the divine world. Thus the Fall, so to say, is effaced, sin and death are destroyed, and all of nature is redeemed, although this transfiguration of the world may not yet be visible to the majority of men in their corporeal condition.

But, in order to understand the meaning of this sacrifice, at once expiatory and transfiguring, in its ultimate depth and the very meaning and purpose of sacrifice generally, we need to know its metaphysical foundation.

As astonishing as it may sound, this foundation is the eternal sacrifice of God. The sacrifice of God is the creation. In a certain way, the creation is the humiliation of God in relation to His Absoluteness. God, who in His Absoluteness is not related to anything outside Himself, becomes a relative-absolute: establishing the being of the creature, He enters into relationship with him. This fact of relating Himself is the sacrifice of the Absolute and the sacrifice of Love for that 'other' that He Himself establishes as created from nothing. Besides, in God the Son, who in one of His aspects, is the principle and the *whole* of creation, 'the first-born of creation' according to the Pauline expression, the Son, as such, is eminently the sacrifice of God. The Incarnation, too, was inscribed in the 'logic', so to say, of the Son of God, with the intention of accomplishing that which had to be, of absolute necessity: to wit, the reintegration of the Creation in the Creator. For the very meaning of sacrifice, as the rite of earth ascending to heaven, is to respond to the divine sacrifice whose movement goes from heaven to earth, and in this way leads all things back to their Divine Principle. Christ effected the return because as God-Man, or Archetypal Man, or Universal Man:[14] 'It is in Him that all things have been created, in heaven and on earth, things visible and invisible ... and all things subsist in Him' (Col. 1: 18–19).' In himself He gathers together the whole of creation which He is able to return to the Father-Origin. 'I am come from the Father and to the Father I return.' And by way of consequence, this becomes true, too,

14. Cf. N. Cabasilas: 'It was for the new man that human nature was created at the beginning.... [Christ] Himself is the Archetype of those who are created ... the Saviour first and alone showed to us the true man, who is perfect' (*The Life in Christ*, Book 6, §12).

of the individual man, who himself is also the mirror and synthesis of creation, the microcosm, and thereby, alone of all creatures, capable also of offering the sacrifice. And of gathering the fruits: 'I have prayed that where I am you also might be.' These two sayings of Christ define what one can call the theanthropic trajectory, in Christ first and then in man.

The Holy Sacrifice of the Mass has no other purpose than to enable us to travel this trajectory, as the following prayer says: 'May these holy offerings, O Almighty God, cleanse us by their mighty power, and make us more pure to approach Him Who is their Author. (Secret of the first Sunday of Advent).'

2

The Holy Mysteries

FROM what we have just said, it will be clear that the sacrifice of Christ extends very much further than is usually suggested by the word, immolation and death not being the whole of sacrifice. To tell the truth, they are not even the essential, although, as we have recalled, they may be necessary for it and indeed are only the condition of passage to another plane of existence, from that of the fallen physical world to the spiritual world. Christ's death is only the prelude to His resurrection, to His birth, as man, in the divine universe where, still as man, He is glorified. It is within this perspective that the doctrine of expiatory and redemptive suffering in the divine-human domain should be understood. Provided it is assumed into the total sacrificial perspective, including death and resurrection, abasement and exaltation, this role of suffering is explained by the fact that the latter, being the wages of sin, like death to which it is related and which it accompanies, tends to detach us from the sensible, phenomenal world. The same goes for asceticism. If this were not so, when one says of God that, 'suffering is acceptable to Him' who 'willed the sufferings of His Son', while losing sight of the final goal of glorification that is the ultimate foundation of sacrifice, one is imagining Him a corrupt and sadistic tyrant.

Thus Christ's death is a quickening death and prelude to resurrection. And this death with a view to glory is the final outcome of what Scripture calls the 'mystery of salvation'. While the latter is an even broader notion than that of sacrifice, even in its widest meaning, sacrifice is nevertheless at once its core and ultimate goal. The mystery of salvation is the revelation of God in the Logos, the Word Incarnate; God revealed Himself to the world in human nature for the salvation of the latter, as St Paul so well expressed when he wrote:

23

[God] made known unto us the mystery of his will, according to his good pleasure which he has purposed in himself: that in the dispensation of the fullness of times he might gather together in one all things in Christ; [this is] the mystery which from the beginning of the world has been hid in God' (Eph. 1:9ff., 3:9).

This mystery is the epiphany of Christ in whom divinity and humanity meet, through whom the Spirit descended to sanctify the earth. It is the Passover of the Lord, death and resurrection, the saving mystery upon which the Church is founded: the mystery that is the source of life, the source of life in the Spirit, transfiguring life.

But salvation is not effected by simple faith in Christ having died once for all. The fact of redemption needs to live in the Church from a mystical and concrete presence at each moment of duration. It is important to insist upon this point. The spiritualization of the idea of sacrifice, leading to a simple movement of personal faith in the sacrifice of Christ accomplished *in illo tempore*, and to the prayer of praise, which is the Protestant position, ruins not only the notion of sacrifice, but the very idea of religion, for the sacrifice celebrated *hic et nunc* is an essential constitutive element of all religion. In fact, such excessive spiritualization risks ending up in the rejection of all form, of every external act, which happened to later Judaism. Religion then cedes its place to an individualistic and subjectivist religious sentimentalism, in which one is occupied more with man than God.

Moreover Christ, before His death, instituted the *rite* which should at each moment perpetuate in a concrete and objective way the mystery of salvation, and transmitted to His disciples the supernatural *powers* for its, the rite's, real accomplishment.

Do this in remembrance of Me; for each time you eat of this bread and drink of this cup, you announce My death and confess My resurrection until My return.... We commemorate Thy death, Lord, we confess Thy resurrection and await Thy second Coming.[1]

Through this rite, the Church, born of the Blood of Christ, is

---

1. Words of consecration in the Syrian Mass.

called to live from this blood, by dying to the world and perpetually rising with Jesus. In one and the same Great Work, Christ and the Church are united in the mystery of salvation; a Great Work in three acts: Baptism, Confirmation and Eucharist. But of these three, the greatest without any possible doubt is the Eucharist. Most assuredly, the eucharistic sacrifice differs greatly from the blood sacrifices of long ago; it is, as the liturgy says, a 'spiritual sacrifice' (*logiki thysia*), but is identified with an external liturgy, the Mass. The latter is a sacred action that man accomplishes outwardly, but that Christ, through the intermediary of the priest, realizes inwardly in each one of us. This sacred action is also called the 'Holy Mysteries' (*tà haghia mystiria, sacra mysteria*). And it is altogether remarkable that the same word *mystirion* simultaneously designates, both the supernatural action of the Son of God in view of humanity's salvation, and the ritual action applying it to man in a visible fashion. The expression 'holy mysteries' is not peculiar to Christianity: it is inherited from ancient Greece where it served to designate the liturgy of certain more or less esoteric cults, like those of Eleusis. These, as opposed to the official cult of the Olympian gods, which assured the security of the City, aimed first of all at assuring the salvation of the individual. Besides, the Greek mysteries belonged to a far larger ensemble of similar cults, such that the word can be applied, *mutatis mutandis*, to a thoroughly universal type of liturgy. The fundamental idea of all the *mysteria* is that of initiation into divine life in view of salvation and immortality. These cults were therefore essentially soteriological. They were founded upon a myth—myth in the etymological sense, that is, a sacred narrative—reporting the deeds and sufferings of a god, close to man, who lived on earth long ago, *in illo tempore*, and participated in human sufferings. Thus Greece presents us with the myth of Dionysius, killed and dismembered by the Titans under the name of Zagreus, while the Greco-Egyptian religion has the myth of Osiris, the principle of Good, killed by his brother Seth, the incarnation of evil, and also dismembered. These sufferings and deaths, though, are in all cases the prelude to a resurrection: Zagreus was resurrected with the name of Dionysius; Osiris was reborn, thanks to his sister-spouse, the powerful goddess Isis. What specifically constitutes the mysteries, however, is the existence of an appropriate rite, also deriving from that primordial time, a rite that is capable of renewing and once again making these deeds and sufferings present, whereby their efficacy for men is perpetuated. These gods performed or suffered an action *in illo tempore* by virtue of which all those believing therein, the *mystes* (Greek *mystis*), entered into an ontological relationship with divinity, re-enacting, in their initiation, his tests and triumphs and thereby obtaining salvation and immortality. Let us add, finally, that this rite nearly always assumes the aspect of a figurative or symbolic dramatic representation according to the case.

In this general outline one will have easily recognized the shape of the Christian liturgy, the liturgy of the mysteries, which is the central activity of our religion. In the eucharistic celebration the two essential elements of Christianity are intimately united: the prayer of praise and thanksgiving and the divine sacrifice. The eucharist is the conjoint action of Christ, through His mystery of death and resurrection, and the ecclesial community participating through the rite in this mystery of salvation.

The mode of this rite of salvation is described as a *memorial*: the Mass is the 'Memorial of the Lord'. This is to say that the Divine Liturgy involves a 'remembering' of the sacrifice of Christ and the whole economy of salvation. 'Do this,' He said, 'in *remembrance* of Me'; and the priest, in the anaphora or canon, embroiders on these divine words by saying, '*Mindful*, therefore, O Lord, not only of the blessed passion of the same Christ, Thy Son, .. we offer unto Thy supreme majesty, of Thy gifts bestowed upon us, etc.' (*Roman Canon*); 'we *commemorate* Thy death' (*Syrian Anaphora*); 'Therefore, *remembering* . . . all that He endured for us: the Cross, the Grave, the Resurrection, etc., . . . Thine own of Thine own we offer to Thee . . . etc.' (*Anaphora of the Byzantine Mass*); 'Christ who was immolated for our salvation has ordered us to *commemorate* His Death; His Tomb and His Resurrection. . . . This sacrifice is the *memorial* of the passion, burial and resurrection of our Lord and Sovereign, Jesus Christ' (*Assyro-Chaldean Mass*). Other liturgies could also be cited. What we see everywhere is the same formula, called the *anamnesis*, (Greek *anamnesis*, 'commemoration', 'remembrance'); and we also see, in examining it, the importance it has in the Mass, for the anamnesis is directly joined to the oblation of the sacrifice, of the Holy Species just consecrated. This amounts to saying that the celebration is done in *remembrance* of the death, the sacrifice of Christ, and His resurrection.

We see from this the danger of false interpretation, which is no empty threat, since such is the interpretation of Protestantism. Calvin, for example, saw the liturgy of the Mass as purely a memorial intended to revive the memory of the blessings of Jesus, to refresh our memory and rekindle piety. The matter needs to be examined closely, for this interpretation, which totally destroys the nature and content of the Mass, is in the process of spreading somewhat everywhere in the Catholic Church of the West. If the Mass is simply this fiction worthy of theatre, or even a commemoration like that of the war dead before the Arc de Triomphe de l'Etoile in Paris, it does not warrant devoting much time to it. One could without much loss have it disappear from Christianity so as to take refuge in a purely inward cult. But this is not the way it is. The Divine Liturgy is the very heart of the Church and the ecclesial community, the irreplaceable source whence it draws the necessary strength to effect salvation, the action in which, as we were saying above, it participates in the mystery of salvation and the person of Christ. We read in St Denis the Areopagite,

> The divine Goodness, [after the fall] wrought a complete change in our nature.... [It] delivered the dwelling place of our souls from the most accursed passion.... Finally [It] showed us a supramundane uplifting and an inspired way of life in shaping ourself to it as fully as lay in our power. This imitation of God, how else are we to achieve it if not by endlessly reminding ourselves of God's sacred works and doing so by way of the sacred hymns and the sacred acts established by the hierarchy? (*Eccl. Hier.* 3, 11–12).

The Protestant conception is totally foreign to the faith of the apostolic Churches of both East and West for whom, in spite of certain theological differences in detail, the Mass is a real sacrifice, effected through the real presence of Christ in the gifts. In the Mass, says the Latin Church, Christ is 'truly, really and substantially' present.[2] Before the consecration, the deacon in the Armenian Mass proclaims, 'Let no catechumens or anyone with doubtful faith, no penitents or the impure approach the Divine Mysteries: the Body of the Lord and Blood of the Redeemer are about to become present here.' And this realization of the presence is identical with the sacrifice. 'O God,' says the Byzantine priest, 'purify my soul and heart ... and make me fit, in the strength of the Holy Spirit, having clothed me with the Grace of the priesthood, to stand before this holy table and here sacrifice Thy holy and pure Body and Thy precious Blood.' [And again: 'Grant, O Lord, that we may worthily approach these Holy Mysteries, for, each time this sacrifice is celebrated in *remembrance* of Thy passion, the work of our redemption is accomplished' (Secret of the ninth Sunday after Pentecost in the Latin Rite). This last prayer perfectly sums up all the authentic theology of the Mass.

In its very terms, however, it invites us to return once again to the word *remembrance,* which needs to be explained in order to understand its harmony with apostolic doctrine. In the Holy Mysteries, Christ makes Himself substantially present; He performs the same sacrifice of expiation and praise as at Calvary. The divine Victim arises in our midst and communion of His Body and Blood associates us ontologically with His sacrifice, His salvation, His person even. This is to say that, as far as the Mass is concerned, the words *remembrance* and *commemorate* do not have the meaning they have in modern languages. And this is because these languages vehicle a culture from which the very notion that these words express in traditional societies[3] is absent, and which we will briefly explain.

Commemoration, in an authentic religious context, is what could be called a *ritual remembrance.* It is the celebration of a divine

---

2. Council of Trent, Sess. 3, Can. 1.

3. We wish to clarify here, once and for all, the meaning of the word 'traditional' that we shall be led to use on many occasions. A society founded on a superhuman *sacred tradition* is *traditional;* a tradition that constitutes the source of its deepest life and from which all its activities flow, the orientation and modalities of which it governs. Everything in such a society assumes, though to different degrees, a sacred character and nothing in it is really profane. In every way it is just the

work upon which a religious community is founded, a celebration that *re-presents*, in the etymological sense of the word, that is to say, *makes present anew*, that divine work whose goal is union with the god and immortality. The ritual recitation of the divine story of the founding of the community 'is not,' as M. Eliade has so well put it, 'a commemoration [in the ordinary sense] of mythic events, but a *reiteration* of them. The protagonists of the myth are made present, one becomes their contemporary.'[4] The ritual recitation takes us out of ordinary time in order to place us again in primordial time when the divine event occurred.

This conception is absolutely universal in all religious contexts. A well-known example is that of Ancient Greece where *Mnemosyne*, that is Memory personified, was the mother of the Muses. We are sometimes astonished at this and ask why poetic and, in general, artistic inspiration was thus made dependent on memory. It is quite simply because memory was taken in the just defined religious sense. Mnemosyne allowed the poet to be present in the divine past, to rejoin the time of ancient events and above all the mystery of origins, of genesis, as Plato explained.[5] The aim of remembrance, for the archaic Greeks, was not to situate events in a temporal frame, but to attain the depth of being, the original, primordial reality, which is equivalent to stepping out of time.[6] Moreover, with Plato, commemoration, or anamnesis (*anamnesis*), an essentially Platonic

---

opposite of a secular society like that of the modern West, in contrast to that of the Middle Ages, which was truly a traditional society. It goes without saying that the epithet *traditional* applies, *mutatis mutandis*, to all human activity; occupations, art, architecture, doctrines etc. From what we have just said, it is obvious that the word *traditional* means something quite different from *traditionalist*.

4. In *Myth and Reality*, 1963, p19 and *passim*. The idea of ritual remembrance, or of commemoration, can, in the case of the Mass, be an allusion to the sacrifice of *minhah* (see above, p8); the portion of the *minhah* that one burnt on the altar was called *azkarah*, that is to say 'commemoration' (from the verb *zakar* 'to remember') and in Greek *anamnesis*, which in Greek exactly expresses the idea of 'memorial'; the term *azkarah* marked the identity of the thing designated thus with that to which the term referred: thus the bread and wine blessed at the Last Supper will in a way become the *azkarah* of the Christic sacrifice.

5. Plato (*Ion*, 535c).

6. See J.P. Vernant, *Myth and Thought Among the Greeks*, 1983, p75 ff.

word and the same designating the action of the Mass, is the spiritual activity leading us from the sensible world, subject to time, to the eternal world of Being.

Ancient Egypt offers us another, more specifically cultural, example. Regarding the ceremonies at the temple of Esna, S. Sauneron writes,

> The divine deed (which is the object of the representations in these ceremonies) only took place once, whether it was the creation of the world, the gathering of Tefnut, the massacre of the rebels or some other event at the beginning. Now, the figurative repetition of these deeds, on their anniversaries, is not an anecdotal recalling of a remote affair; it is *an act having full power, which through its ritual execution recreates the event and its consequences.*[7]

With regard to us, the death and resurrection of Christ are archetypes repeated in the liturgical action, and by participating in this action we rejoin the archetypes. The Mass is not an *evocation* of these archetypes, focused on communicating the effects of the sacrifice of Christ; it is an efficacious *reproduction* of and introduces us directly into the event; it makes us contemporaries of Christ, of His deed and His person. And thereby we attain to the 'knowledge' of which the Gospel speaks, which is *contact with the divine*. Without the Divine Liturgy, the redemption would be of the past; through the liturgy we enter into the original mystery. The officiant reproduces exactly what Christ did and said and in this act and word the same thing happens as at the beginning in the archetypal event. Better still, the mystical drama is, moreover, anticipation of the life of the Beyond: 'May this offering, O Lord, about to be dedicated to Thy holy Name, purify us and make us advance day by day in the practice of a heavenly life (Secret of the second Sunday after Pentecost in the Latin Rite).' On the other hand, and we need to insist upon this, it is not only the original deed, the archetypal act, that is reproduced, it is also the original actor who is made, or rather

7. S. Sauneron, *Les fêtes religieuses d'Esna*, 1962, pp 60–61.

makes himself present in the ritual celebration.[8] 'Look down, O Lord Jesus Christ our God,' says the priest,

> [and] come to sanctify us, Thou Who sittest on high with the Father, and art here invisibly present with us. And do Thou deign by Thy mighty hand to give to us of Thine Immaculate Body and of Thy Precious Blood, and through us to all the people' (Prayer of Inclination of the Byzantine Mass).

This real presence of Christ in the offerings, in the bread and wine, as also His real sacrificial action, could obviously not be procured solely through the fact of liturgical words and gestures if these were but words and gestures in the ordinary sense. It was said above that the liturgical act consists in a *ritual* recitation of the archetypal and primordial event, in the present case, the recital of the eucharistic institution at the Last Supper on Maundy Thursday. The meaning and importance of the word 'ritual' needs to be thoroughly understood. A rite, in the strict sense we have in mind, is a word or gesture or collection of words and gestures, of *supra-human origin*, to which a *spiritual energy* is attached capable of realizing what the words and gestures signify. It can, moreover, only be performed by a qualified agent, that is to say one invested, by the same divine authority that created the rite, with a particular *power*, the power, precisely, to perform this rite. Such is the case with all Christian sacraments, and in particular the Eucharist:

> He (Christ) himself said: 'This is my body. This is my blood.' He himself commanded the Apostles to do this, . . . 'Do this,' he said, 'in remembrance of me'. He would not have given the command unless he had been going to give them the power to enable them to do this. What then is this power? It is the Holy Spirit, the power from on high which has strengthened the Apostles.[9]

---

8. It is important, today perhaps more than in the past, to see clearly that this 'real presence' in the material of the sacrifice is essential in the great religions. Thus in the animal sacrifice of Hinduism, a portion of the victim, called *ida*, is reserved, over which the priest pronounces an invocation (similar to the epiclesis of the Christian Mass) as a result of which the divinity is actually incarnated in the offering.

9. N. Cabasilas, *A Commentary on the Divine Liturgy*, 28, 2.

In the Apostolic Churches, the priest has inherited this power through an uninterrupted transmission, which radically distinguishes him from the Protestant minister. The latter is incapable of realizing a presence of the sacred from the fact that he no longer possesses the *operative power*, because of the break, in his confession, in the apostolic succession. We shall not dwell any longer on this question of *powers*, and would not even have mentioned it, it being so obvious in Christianity, had we not thought it necessary, since such matters are at present somewhat lost to sight. We also wished to show clearly that the conception of archetype and repetition in worship, and of the powers of the officiant, is not peculiar to Christianity, but belongs to the very structure of every true religious institution, and all religious anthropology. This is so because it answers to the profound expectation and fundamental needs of man, who, in the normal state, demands a total and profound religious experience. Not satisfied with words, or content with a sentimental and moralizing idealism, he wants an effective and real contact with the divinity.

On the other hand, it would perhaps be advisable to devote some time to a more difficult question: that of how the ritual remembrance whose functioning we have recalled is able to operate. When we said that, through such ritual remembrance, one rejoined the archetypal event and actor, it could be asked how the actual *time-leap* is realized, taking us from the moment in time where we find ourselves to that primordial moment of the original event. How can the sacrifice of Christ be reproduced at each Mass, and how, to take up the terms used earlier, do we, at a precise moment of history, rejoin His person in the act of His sacrifice realized once, *in illo tempore*?

Because they envisage the problem from a purely temporal point of view, the majority of attempted explanations advanced by theologians are very unconvincing. The only truly satisfactory explanation is that furnished by the metaphysical point of view, which is totally disengaged from temporality.

Some theologians, however, have clearly perceived where one should start if one is to understand things. They explain our problem by relating the Mass to the heavenly liturgy; thus we have Monsieur Olier who in the seventeenth century wrote:

In order to understand the mystery of the most holy sacrifice of the Mass ... one needs to know that this sacrifice is the sacrifice of heaven. ... There is a sacrifice in Paradise, which is simultaneously offered on earth, with the only difference that its presentation here below is veiled.[10]

The author is of course evoking the great scene glimpsed by St John in his Apocalypse: the sacrificed, but living Lamb on a throne, the 24 Elders worshipping it while playing on harps and burning incense, and the multitude of angels as well as all the creatures singing its praises and the eternal *Amen* (Apoc. 5:6–14). Understanding the sacrifice of the Mass in this way is, moreover, and let us be explicit, not a personal theory involving only theologians. It is attested by the very oldest liturgies, in which we find prayers such as this:

Lift your eyes towards the heavenly realities and contemplate the mysteries now celebrated: the seraphim, in respectful awe stand before Christ's Throne of Glory, chanting the praises of the offered Body, the mixed Cup. And here below, the people implore and the priest beseeches and requests mercy for the whole world (Prayer after the consecration in the Assyro-Chaldean Mass).

And again: 'O Holy Trinity, receive from my sinful hands this sacrifice that I offer on the heavenly altar of the Word' (Syrian Mass). Besides, it is not only to St John that similar texts are referring. We find the idea of celestial sacrifice under another form in an already cited passage from St Paul's Epistle to the Hebrews, where he tells us that Christ, at the time of His Ascension, rose to Heaven to be the supreme Pontiff there. Like the High Priest of the Jews on the Day of Expiation, He entered the celestial sanctuary as Man—Perfect Man, to be sure—bringing His own Blood in order to intercede for the multitude of men (Heb. 9:15–28).

Thus the Mass has its prototype in the heavenly sacrifice of the Lamb described by the *Apocalypse*. It is vain to object, as some with a profane point of view do, that this way of conceiving things is simply

---

10. Cited in Gaby, *Le sacrifice dans l'école française de spiritualité*, Paris, 1951.

a projection of the earthly liturgy, which one thus imagines as unfolding in heaven. In fact, for the pneumatic, the inverse is true. He *knows* that the visible liturgy is only the symbolic refraction, on the corporeal plane upon which man moves during terrestrial existence, of the invisible reality On-High, even as music is only the approximate expression, as Marcel de Corte has said, of an essential silence. The Scriptural texts cited use a sensible form to describe a spiritual reality, and present as a temporal unfolding something which, in reality, has never ceased to exist and belongs to eternity. This emerges clearly in another essential passage of the *Apocalypse*, where we read that the Lamb was 'slain from the foundation of the world' (Apoc. 13:8). And also in a passage from St Peter saying that Christ is 'a lamb without blemish and without spot; who verily was foreordained before the foundation of the world, but was manifest in these last times for you' (1 Pet. 1:19). Such terms rejoin the teaching of St Paul on 'the mystery [of Christ] which hath been hid from generations' (Col. 1:27). The Mass is not the *repetition* or *reproduction* of the historical act that was the sacrifice of Calvary, which is moreover impossible. It is not even, at bottom, the *representation*, the term we used above that was valid as a first approximation, but which no more corresponds exactly to the reality than do the others. The consecration by the priest which effects the sacrifice is, more precisely, *the visible manifestation of an eternal act*; it tears the 'illusory' veil of the conditions of space and time that separate the spirit of man from the contemplation of eternal realities. For what the texts cited above teach us in a symbolic form is that the sacrifice of Christ is an eternal act. As soon as one envisages the matter from the metaphysical point of view, all the difficulties of explanation disappear. From this point of view time does not exist, it has only an 'illusory' existence: time only possesses some reality in relation to terrestrial existence. For God, time does not exist. He possesses His Being and all His existence in the 'indivisible present', the *atomon nyn* of Aristotle, and all His acts take place simultaneously. All His operations outside of Himself, which is to say the creation, are performed in one and the same eternal instant; as Meister Eckhart said: 'God creates the entire world *now*, in *this instant*. Everything God created six thousand years ago and when He created the world, He creates instantaneously now ... there where time never enters... He creates the world and all things in this present Now.'[11] The different divine operations and the different events *are manifested* in successive, temporal mode, but essentially everything is already done, everything has already happened from all eternity. Time, according to Plato's admirable formula, is nothing but 'the moving image of eternity' (*aionos ikon kinitis*). Everything happens as though the events, gathered in a single point, were then deployed, projected upon a circle with a moving circumference, which would be time. This image is moreover traditional and corresponds to the nature of things; time, says Boethius, following Plato, is a (great) circumference the central (fixed) point of which is eternity.[12] Thus the liturgy celebrated at any one moment is only the *hic et nunc* visible form of the timeless, eternal Mass of Heaven, described by the *Apocalypse*.[13] The celestial archetype of the liturgy is the true liturgy, always present, perpetually in act. The visible earthly Mass is only the medium through which we enter into relationship with, and share in, the heavenly Liturgy. Finally, the sacrifice itself on Calvary, as an historical fact, is only a manifestation—at an extraordinary degree, to be sure—on earth, of the eternal sacrifice of the 'Lamb immolated from the beginning', which is precisely the heavenly Liturgy.

This eternal sacrifice is that of the Word, always and forever, priest of His Father to whom He constantly offers the infinite sacrifice: He is Himself this sacrifice as the substantial Glory of the Father who returns to His principle though the substantial Love of the Holy Spirit. Simultaneously, the Son offers the Father homage in the name of the whole of Creation in as much as He is 'the firstborn of every creature (*prototokos pasis ktiseos*): for by him were all things created, that are in heaven, and that are in earth, visible and invisible. . . .' (Col. 1:15–16).

11. Ed. Pfeiffer, pp190, 192, 207, 266, 297. Cf. Plutarch, *On the 'E' at Delphi*, 20; God is 'the sole Being that fills the Always with a single Now.' In passing, let us note that this point of view allows for the resolution of otherwise insoluble theological difficulties, like the relationships of human freedom to Providence.

12. Boethius, *The Consolation of Philosophy*, 4, 6, 15–16. The image is taken up again by Ruysbroek, *De septem custo diis*, 19.

13. See above, p39.

Thus, we see ourselves returning to what was already explained on the universal character of the sacrifice. The eternal Son offers the Father a double oblation: His Person and the universe, and this double aspect of the oblation answers to what we have called the Sacrifice of the Divinity. God 'issues' from His Absoluteness and engenders *ad intra* His Son and, through the Son *prototokos*, produces *ad extra* the universe with all its creatures. To this Sacrifice of God, this 'issuing forth of God', the Sacrifice of Creation should reply, and thereby 're-enter' God. We have seen that this is the metaphysical basis of all sacrifice and have said that the Sacrifice of Golgotha eminently possesses this cosmic quality. It transfers the whole of the spatio-temporal world together with man who is its summation to the divine world, thereby effecting that reintegration of the whole of Nature to which St Paul alludes. We have also said that the Mass shares this cosmic dimension, and it is upon this aspect of the Divine Liturgy that we would like to dwell a little in concluding this chapter, for this is where the extent of the 'Mystery of Christ' truly appears with all its force. 'We offer Thee this spiritual worship for the whole universe', says the priest in the Byzantine Mass. The Divine Liturgy is first of all a service of praise for creation, it is the office of the cosmos turned to its eternal Principle. According to the Psalmist, Nature unanimously declares the glory of God (Psalm 18); but nature is unconscious. The praise of the world needs to pass through the heart of man in order to become living and intelligent harmony. Man is the consciousness of the world, for he is a microcosm, a summary of the world. As St Gregory, for example, says,

Man has something in common with every creature . . . he for whom everything on earth was created and to whom, at least by way of a certain similitude, nothing is foreign.[14]

And Bossuet:

Man has a spirit and heart greater than the world, to the end that, contemplating the entire universe and gathering it together in himself, he might offer, sanctify and consecrate it to the living God. So much so is this the case, that it is only in order that he

14. *Hom. in Ev.* 292 (P L 76, 121, 413).

might, through a holy love, be visible nature's priest and wor-
shipper of invisible and intellectual nature, that he is the
former's contemplator and mysterious abridgement.[15]

In the Divine Liturgy, man is creation's precentor before God.
This hymn of the universe was developed at length in the ancient
anaphoras, in particular the anaphora of the *Apostolic Constitutions*,
where the officiant reviewed all aspects of the created world in order
to give thanks to God for them before consecrating the offerings:

You are He who framed the heaven as an arch, and stretch it out
like the covering of a tent, and founded the earth upon nothing
by Your mere will; who fixed the firmament, and prepare the
night and the day; who brought the light out of Your treasures,
and on its departure brought on darkness, for the rest of the living creatures that move up and down in the world; who
appointed the sun in heaven to rule over the day, and the moon
to rule over the night, and inscribed in heaven the choir of stars
to praise Your glorious majesty.

You made the water for drink and for cleansing, the air in which
we live for respiration and the affording of sounds, by the means
of the tongue, which strikes the air, and the hearings which co-
operates therewith, so as to perceive speech when it is received by
it, and falls upon it.

You made fire for our consolation in darkness, for the supply of
our want, and that we might be warmed and enlightened by it.

You separated the great sea from the land, and rendered the
former navigable and the latter fit for walking, and replenished
the former with small and great living creatures, and filled the
latter with the same, both tame and wild; furnished it with various plants, and crown it with herbs, and beautify it with flowers,
and enrich it with seeds.

You ordained the great deep, and on every side made a mighty
cavity for it, which contains seas of salt waters heaped together,

15. Second Sermon on the Annunciation.

yet You every way bounded them with barriers of the smallest sand; who sometimes dost raise it to the height of mountains by the winds, and sometimes dost smooth it into a plain; sometimes dost enrage it with a tempest, and sometimes dost still it with a calm, that it may be easy to seafaring men in their voyages.

You encompassed this world, which was made by You through Christ, with rivers, and water it with currents, and moisten it with springs that never fail, and bound it round with mountains for the immovable and secure consistence of the earth. . . .

You have replenished Your world, and adorned it with sweet-smelling and with healing herbs, with many and various living creatures, strong and weak, for food and for labor, tame and wild; with the noises of creeping things, the sounds of various sorts of flying creatures; with the circuits of the years, the numbers of months and days, the order of the seasons, the courses of the rainy clouds, for the production of the fruits and the support of living creatures. You have also appointed the station of the winds, which blow when commanded by You.[16]

With the Eucharist, says St Irenaeus, we offer the first fruits of creation: in Christ the entire creation is recapitulated and offered to God.[17] These first fruits are the offerings, the bread and wine, which are a gift from God and which should, after a certain fashion, return to Him, therefore be offered to Him. And they are offered in and through Christ who, as the divine Word, is the immediate author of Creation. This meaning of the offerings emerges very clearly from the formulae, variable in their forms, but essentially the same in their content, that the priest pronounces in all the anaphoras of the West as of the East:

Thine own of Thine own we offer Thee (Byzantine Mass). We offer Thy supreme Majesty the very gift we have received from Thee. . . . It is through Him [Christ] that Thou doest ceaselessly

16. In A. Hamman, *Prières des premiers chrétiens*, 1952, no. 168.
17. St Irenaeus, *Adv. Haer.* 3, 18, 1; (19, 3; 21, 10).

create all these blessings, that Thou doest sanctify and vivify them and give them to us (Roman Canon).[18]

This offering of the first fruits of nature has as its first aim, then, to return to God what has come from Him. But the second aim, which moreover derives from the first and is its consequence, is to obtain anew from God these very gifts that one offers to Him. There is no need to minimize, and even less to despise, this aspect of the Mass in the name of a hyper-spirituality. It is certain that the Sacrifice of the Mass, like many other types of sacrifice besides, aims in part to ensure material prosperity. The great litanies recited at the beginning of the Mass (they have practically disappeared from the Latin Rite, except in the Office of Good Friday), include supplications in this sense:

> For seasonable weather, for the abundance of the fruits of the earth, and for peaceful times, let us pray to the Lord (Byzantine Mass); Through this sacrifice accord us favorable weather, fertile fields and a prompt healing of all sicknesses (Armenian Mass); Accept this sacrifice for the living and the peace of the world, for the cycle of the seasons, that it may be fecund and accomplished according to Thy Will (Assyro-Chaldean Mass).

But if the Latin liturgy is not as explicit in the Ordinary of the Mass, requests of this sort are none the less implicitly included in the sacramental formulae of the Offertory and Canon, cited above, which relate expressly to the gifts of nature, and then—explicitly this time—in the Lord's Prayer: 'Give us this day our daily bread.'

This 'temporal' aspect of the sacrifice is not at all contradictory to its 'spiritual' aspect, the two being, moreover, complementary, for there is no opposition of this sort, neither in man nor in the world, since *everything* comes from the Divinity. For every religious spirit, in all known religious forms, one of the aims, among others, of the sacrifice has been to ensure the fertility of the earth, an indispensable condition of human life. Why? Because the celebration of the sacrifice, which to this end should also be perpetual, maintains the

18. Cf. St Paul, *Col.* 1, 15–20: '. . . for by him were all things created, etc.'

endless 'current of prosperity' that descends from heaven like the fertilizing rain and sunlight, which passing into the plants and animals, becomes our food, then returns to heaven, symbolically in the smoke of the consumed offering, and more spiritually in the Christian offering. Heaven showers its gifts upon the earth and the earth returns them to heaven; the offering raised by the officiant ascends On-High, whence the blessing descends anew Here-Below: in this way the circuit of energy, the vital current, is maintained, activated, or re-established. Under this aspect the sacrifice is the actualization of the vital power itself. Why should this be astonishing, since God and, more especially, the Divine Word is He 'in whom there was Life' and 'through whom all things were made' (John 1:3 and 4). The purpose of the sacrifice in this domain is to maintain cosmic equilibrium. The idea was particularly developed and brought to light in the ancient Egyptian ritual,[19] but is included in all sacrifice. Always threatened—as we know only too well—this equilibrium can be maintained or re-established only by God, 'who upholds all things by the word of his power' (Heb. 1:3). This idea that God is the 'link' supporting all things is often forgotten in our day. It is, however, magnificently expressed in a number of liturgical hymns, and, for example, in the hymns of the daily office in the Latin Rite:

> *God, the power that upholds all creation,*
> *While remaining immutable in Thyself,*
> *And yet determining in due order*
> *the successive changes of the light of day...*
> (Hymn of None)

> *Mighty ruler, true God,*
> *Who governs the course of things,*
>
> ....
>
> *Extinguish the flames of strife,*
> *Keep far from us the heat of passion,*
> *Grant health to our bodies.*
> (Hymn of Sext)

19. See in particular Ph. Derchain, *Le Papyrus Salt*, 825.

But we nevertheless have here only the lower degree of this cosmic aspect of the Holy Sacrifice. In its most elevated sense, it is the operation whereby the God-Man, 'The Firstborn of Creation' leads the whole universe back to God, raising it from the visible to the invisible plane. Through the Eucharist man re-assumes the original power through which God granted life to the world, restoring life to the world through His Death and Resurrection. God resurrects man and the world in their original purity and saves them from Evil. 'Christ was hung on the Cross,' St Irenaeus writes, 'in order to unite the universe in Himself', because the Cross itself, as we shall see further on, is the symbol of the universe. St Andrew of Crete, following St Paul, also sings in one of his hymns, 'O Cross, reconciliation of the cosmos, boundary of the earthly expanse, *height* of heaven, *depths* of the earth, bond of the creation, *extent* of everything visible, *breadth* of the universe' (Cf. Eph. 3:18–19). Redemption not only involves the reconciliation of man but, as expressed by this hymn, that of the entire cosmos of which man is the summary, and himself the individual reflection of the God-Man. If, for the individual man, salvation is henceforth assured, the cosmos, on the other hand, is not, alas, effectively redeemed and 'nature groans' (Rom. 8:22). However, the redemption of the cosmos is virtually acquired, and if the effects are not apparent to it yet, it is nonetheless certainly returned to its primordial purity, identical to that of the 'new earth and new heaven' announced by the *Apocalypse*. Evoking the drama of Calvary, a Latin Good Friday hymn expresses it thus:

> *The thorns, nails and spear*
> *Pierced His body so dear,*
> *Whence flowed water and blood:*
> *All was washed in that flood,*
> *Earth, sea, heaven and hell.*

The ancient liturgies integrated this cosmic aspect of the redemptive mystery. This is normal, for every traditional rite always refers to the origin, to primordial times, to the original creative instant, because every sacred action draws its efficacy from its coincidence with the instant when the supernatural power that established it sprang forth. This is why a sacred rite nearly always includes an account of cosmogony or creation;[20] such an account is found in the ancient Christian liturgies, as can be seen in the extracts from one of them reproduced above. This is because the restoration cannot be accomplished except through a recapitulation, that is to say a return of the whole story of creation to its beginning. The majority of anaphoras, in becoming shorter, have considerably reduced this cosmogonic account, even doing away with it, as in the Roman Canon. They have only kept the mention of the creation of man but, starting from there, still retrace the history of humanity ending up at the redemption and giving a glimpse into the Parousia and the Kingdom of Heaven, for, once again, it is all of this that the sacrifice of the Mass represents. Among current living liturgies, the anaphora of St Basil, in the Byzantine rite, offers the most complete and magnificent expression of the commemoration of the history of man and the world. We shall now reproduce most of it by way of closing this chapter, for which it will be the perfect summary.

The Anaphora of St Basil:

O thou who art Master, Lord God, Father Almighty, adorable, it is truly meet and right, and befitting the magnificence of thy holiness that we should praise thee, hymn thee, bless thee, worship thee, give thanks unto thee and glorify thee, the only truly existing God, and offer unto thee with a broken heart and the spirit of humility this our rational worship, for thou art He that hath bestowed upon us the knowledge of thy truth. And who is sufficient to speak of thy mighty acts, to make all thy praises to be heard, or to declare all thy wonders at every time? O Master of all, Lord of heaven and earth, and of all creation both visible and invisible, who sittest upon the throne of glory, and lookest upon the depths, who art without beginning, invisible, incomprehensible, uncircumscript, immutable, the Father of our Lord Jesus Christ, our great God and Saviour, our hope, who is the image of thy goodness, the seal of equal type, in Himself showing forth

---

20. This is clearly seen in the nocturnal office of Easter when the first chapters of Genesis are proclaimed. We have analyzed this office in our book *The Symbolism of the Christian Temple*, p143 ff.

thee, the Father, Living Word, true God, the Wisdom before the ages, the Life, Sanctification, Power, the true Light, through whom the Holy Spirit was revealed, the Spirit of truth, the Gift of adoption, the Pledge of an inheritance to come, the First-fruits of eternal good things, the life-creating Power, the Fountain of sanctification, by whom enabled, every rational and intelligent creature doth worship thee, and send up to thee everlasting doxology, for all things are thy servants. Yea, Angels and Archangels, Thrones, Dominions, Principalities, Authorities, Powers, and the many-eyed Cherubim praise thee. Round about thee stand the Seraphim, one with six wings and another with six wings, and with twain they cover their faces, and with twain their feet, and with twain they fly, calling out to one another with unceasing voices and unending doxologies, singing the hymn of victory, crying, calling, and saying:

Holy, Holy, Holy, Lord of Sabaoth.
Heaven and earth are full of thy glory,
Hosanna in the highest.
Blessed is He that cometh in the name of the Lord,
Hosanna in the highest.

With these blessed Powers, O Master, Lover of man, we sinners also do cry out and say, Holy art thou, in truth, and all-holy, and there is no measure to the magnificence of thy holiness, and holy art thou in all thy works, for in righteousness and true judgment hast thou brought about all things for us. When thou hadst fashioned man, taking dust from the earth, and hadst honored him with thine own image, O God, thou didst set him in a paradise of plenty, promising him life immortal and the enjoyment of eternal good things in the observance of thy commandments. But when he disobeyed thee, the true God, who had created him, and was led astray by the deceit of the serpent, and was slain by his own trespasses, thou didst banish him, in thy righteous judgment, O God, from Paradise into this world, and didst turn him back to the earth from which he was taken, dispensing salvation for him through regeneration, which is in thy Christ Himself. Yet thou didst not turn thyself away till the end from thy creature which thou hadst made, O Good One, neither didst thou forget the work of thy hands, but thou didst look upon him in divers manners, through thy tenderhearted mercy. Thou didst send forth prophets; thou hast wrought mighty works through the saints who in every generation have been well-pleasing unto thee; thou didst speak to us by the mouths of thy servants the prophets, who foretold to us the salvation which was to come; thou didst give the Law as an help; thou didst appoint guardian angels. And when the fullness of time was come, thou didst speak unto us through thy Son Himself, by whom also thou madest the ages; Who, being the brightness of thy glory, and the express image of thy person, and upholding all things by the word of His power, deemed it not robbery to be equal to thee, the God and Father. But albeit He was God before the ages, yet He appeared upon earth and sojourned among men; and was incarnate of a holy Virgin, and did empty Himself, taking on the form of a servant, and becoming conformed to the body of our humility, that He might make us conformed to the image of His glory. For as by man sin entered the world, and by sin death, so thine Only-begotten Son, Who is in thy bosom, God and Father, was well-pleased to be born of a woman, the holy Theotokos and Ever-virgin Mary, to be born under the Law, that He might condemn sin in His flesh, that they who were dead in Adam might be made alive in thy Christ Himself, and, becoming a citizen in this world, and giving ordinances of salvation, He removed from us the delusion of idols and brought us unto a knowledge of thee, the true God and Father, having won us unto Himself for His own people, a royal priesthood, a holy nation, and being purified with water, and sanctified by the Holy Spirit, He gave Himself a ransom to Death, whereby we were held, sold under sin. And having descended into hell through the Cross, that He might fill all things with Himself, He loosed the pains of death, and rose again from the dead on the third day, making a way for all flesh unto the resurrection from the dead—for it was not possible that the Author of life should be holden of corruption— that He might be the first-fruits of those who have fallen asleep, the first-born from the dead, that He might be all, being first in all. And, ascending into heaven, He sat down at the right hand of thy majesty on high, and He shall return to render unto everyone according to his works. And He hath left with us as remembrances of His saving Passion these Things which we have set forth according to His commandment. For when He was about to go forth to His voluntary, and celebrated, and life-creating death, in the night in which He gave Himself up for the life of the world, He took bread in His holy and immaculate hands, and when He had shown it unto thee, the God and Father, and given thanks, and blessed it, and hallowed it, and broken it, He gave it to His holy disciples and apostles, saying: Take, eat, this is my Body, which is broken for you for the forgiveness of sins. Likewise, having also taken the cup of the fruit of the vine, and mingled it (with water), and given thanks, and blessed and hallowed it, He gave it to His holy disciples and apostles, saying: Drink ye all of this; this is my Blood of the New Testament, which is shed for you and for many, for the forgiveness of sins. Do this in remembrance of me, for as often as ye shall eat this Bread and drink of this Cup, ye do proclaim my death and confess my resurrection.

Wherefore, O Master, we also remembering His saving Passion and life-creating Cross, His three-day burial, and resurrection from the dead, His ascension into heaven, and sitting down at thy right hand, God and Father, and His glorious and fearful second coming, ... Thine own of thine own we offer unto thee on behalf of all and for all.

3

The Divine Liturgy

SHOWING in the previous chapter that the Mass is a commemoration and, more exactly, a 'ritual remembrance', we devoted ourselves to recalling above all the nature of this remembrance, and even more, its realistic, efficacious and operative character. Now it is time to explore its content, manner of unfolding, and structure.

To clear the ground, we shall start by recalling the most obvious structural feature of the Mass, which will lead to a recollection and study of its origin, from where in turn we shall go more deeply into the very substance of the rite and its inner structure.

Everyone knows that the Mass is ordinarily divided into two large parts. The first, which goes from the beginning to the reading of the Gospel and the homily is called—and very improperly so, moreover, but we shall return to this—'the Preparation'. The second, which comprises the rest of the sacred office: the offertory, consecration, and communion, is the Mass properly so-called, to use the usual terminology.

The first part is made up essentially of readings and songs of praise: in it the assembly of the faithful plays the principal role, whereas in the second part, it is more the priest who does so. The whole of the first part is an adaptation of synagogue worship, in which ever since the destruction of the Temple readings and prayers replaced sacrificial worship: readings and prayers oriented in part to the expectation of the New Covenant—the work of the Messiah—and the Great Sacrifice that would seal it. Even after the reconstruction of the Temple, this cult continued, not only beyond, but also in Jerusalem, and is still in existence. But in order to properly understand the adaptation of synagogue worship to Christianity, one needs to go back further, to before the destruction of the Temple and recall what the 'Assembly of the faithful' or the *qahal* was. The *qahal* was the convocation of the people to hear the word of God and give Him an official response, and was presented as a ceremony in four parts:

1) the convocation of the people,
2) who listened to the solemn reading of the divine Word,
3) accepted it with jubilation, praise and prayer, and then
4) renewed and confirmed their covenant with God through the sacrifice.[1]

Now what did the Apostles do? They summoned the new chosen people in order to gather them together, let them hear the Word of God and seal the new covenant through the Great Sacrifice at last realized.

To understand the Mass properly, one also needs to remember the Jewish liturgy of meals, and especially the paschal meal, the more so since it was the setting chosen by Christ Himself for the institution of His sacrament. In a way the paschal meal constituted a family version—narrowed down as a result—of the great *qahal* outlined above. In pious communities (the *haburoth*) at the time of Jesus, liturgical meals, modeled on the paschal meal, were celebrated on the eve of the Sabbath and the great feasts. The way in which these meals unfolded also enables us to understand the unfolding of the Last Supper on Maundy Thursday. Before the meal, kinds of hors-d'oeuvre—what today in the East is called the *meze*—were served and cups of wine were circulated, all of which were blessed. The 'first cup' at the Last Supper, mentioned by St Luke (22:17), was one of these. Then the guests washed their hands with perfumed water and the meal properly so-called began. It opened with the solemn *breaking of bread* by the head of the family or community, who pronounced the following formula of thanksgiving: 'Blessed art Thou, Lord, who caused bread to be produced from the earth.' It is doubtless at this moment that Christ consecrated the bread. The different dishes were then brought in and blessed, followed by the cups of wine, each participant blessing his

1. See, for example, 2 Kings 23.

own cup. At the end of the meal, the last cup was solemnly blessed by the head of the community: 'Blessed art Thou, Lord... who created the fruit of the vine.' This rite was preceded by the rite of the lamps, which were brought in, and of the incense, and by the washing of hands a second time. The latter Jesus replaced with the washing of the Apostles' feet. The solemn rite of the last cup, in which one mixed water with the wine, was accompanied by a great thanksgiving (*eucharistia*), in which the head of the community recalled the benefits of God, material and spiritual, since the exodus from Egypt. It is here that Jesus consecrated the wine sealing the new covenant. Following in His footsteps, the first Christian communities practised a type of celebration made up of the *kerygma*, or the announcing of the Word of Jesus convoking the people of God; the praises of the assembly invoking this Word made flesh, through the prayers inherited from the synagogue; and finally, the sacrifice, 'the breaking of bread', the proclamation of the Death and Resurrection of the Saviour, indefinitely sealing the New Covenant across time, 'until He come, again.'[2]

It was not only the general structure of synagogue worship and of these meals—sacrificial meals, not simple feasts of friendship let it be remembered—that passed into the Mass where one even finds traces of these rites in the detail of hymns and formulae. The greeting of the priest to the faithful: 'The Lord be with you', in the West, and in the East, 'Peace be with you', comes directly from the Jews. The first formula is that of Boaz addressing his reapers (Ruth 2:4; cf. 2 Chron. 15:2; Judg. 6:12), the second is the traditional greeting *shalom lakem* (cf. Arabic *as-salamu alaikum*). The conclusion of the lesser doxologies at the end of prayers, 'unto ages of ages', is the exact copy of the Hebrew liturgical formula *min ha-olam ad ha-olam*. As for *Amen* and *Alleluia*, preserved in their original language, they are directly connected with these just recalled rites. As is the case now in the Mass, *Amen* served as an acclamation after the doxology, expressing the adherence of the people to the praise. *Alleluia* deserves a lot more attention than we can give it here; it certainly assumes a much greater importance in the office than is apparent at

2. See Acts 2:42.

first sight. Most people are unaware of, or do not remember its meaning: it is considered to be a cry of joy, which is not untrue, but in fact the formula has quite another application. *Hallelu-yah* means: 'Praise God', or 'God be praised'; it comes, precisely, from the *Hallel*, the suite of Psalms[3] chanted at the paschal meal, recalling the marvels performed by God; after each verse the people cried out *Hallelu-yah*. The practice remains in the Mass in the three Alleluias chanted likewise after the few verses from the Psalms that occur before the Gospel. This invocation of the Name of God assumes all its importance when considered in the light of one of the verses of Psalm 115—one of the Hallel hymns—that the Latin priest says at the moment of his communion. 'What shall I render unto the Lord for all his benefits toward me? I will take the cup of salvation, and call upon the Name of the Lord.' Which means that there is a very close link between the eating of the Bread of Life and the invocation of the Name of God. The examination of this idea, however, will take us too far afield: our remarks, at any rate, will be enough to make some people reflect.

Finally, there is a last formula of thanksgiving preserved by us from the synagogal office, which in all liturgies is none other than the solemn beginning of the Anaphora (called 'the Preface' in the West). 'It is meet and right to hymn Thee, to bless Thee, to praise Thee, to give thanks unto Thee, and to worship Thee in every place of Thy dominion, etc.' In fact, after the commemoration of God's activity in behalf of His people and the chanting of the *shema* (Deut. 6:4 ff.), the president said, 'Sincere and worthy, faithful and unchangeable, just and truthful … is the promise that has been made to us.' He then moved to the thanksgiving, which included, as is the case in the Mass too, an evocation of the heavenly hosts and the chanting of the *Sanctus*.

From all we have just said it is quite certain then that the setting and general orientation, including a good number of the formulae of the Mass, come straight from the Jewish liturgy, both synagogal and paschal. The matter has today been amply demonstrated, definitively putting paid to the thesis, formerly supported by rationalistic

3. Psalms 113–118.

49

and hellenistic criticism above all, which derived the whole liturgy of the Mass from the ancient mysteries, Greek, Oriental, or Greco-Oriental, about which we have already spoken. Having said that, one should not go to the opposite extreme, which could be called that of the Judaizing theologians and liturgists, who emphasize the Hebraic character of the divine liturgy to such an extent that they refuse it any connection—we expressly say: any connection—with the mystery religions in question. But there is, for all that, a primary fact that should catch their attention: that is the liturgy's use of the principal terms of the Greek vocabulary of the mysteries, starting with the designation of the Mass as *ta hiera mystiria*, 'The Holy Mysteries'. But this is not the essential point. From the analysis one can make of the synagogal office and the Jewish liturgy of the Passover, it is evident that the content and spirit of these rites are radically different from the Christian rite. The Jewish rites appear to be the expression of a profound religious spirit, to be sure, but essentially attached to the things of the earth, to tangible and material benefits. Doubtless, among these benefits one also includes the fact of monotheism, faith in a unique and transcendent God. But therein precisely lies the point of rupture between the two religions and rites. The essential of the Christian rite of the Mass, to wit the eating of the dead and resurrected god and the assimilation of the faithful to the god resulting therefrom, is totally foreign to Judaism, at least in its exoteric form,[4] where the profession of such ideas appeared to be the height of sacrilege. These ideas are on the other hand the very ones associated with the ancient mysteries. There again, it is true that the Judaizers, to support their thesis, present a totally inexact conception of the ancient mysteries. We are thinking particularly of a celebrated theologian, who, treating of these problems, and claiming to follow the latest research, calls the ancient mysteries 'magical and agrarian rites'. This point of view is completely out of date today. For example, the findings of K. Kerenyi or Ch. Picard on Eleusis, in particular, have refuted this theory also held by P.-J. Nilsson, and demonstrated the authentic spiritual value of the Eleusinian religion. And as for

---

4. But it is difficult to know the Jewish esoterism of the Old Testament. In any case, we in no way intend to address this problem here.

the mysteries of Isis, we who have devoted numerous years of research to this subject, find the judgment of the author in question laughable. In fact, we are not claiming that the Christian rite *comes* from the ancient mysteries. In its outward form it certainly comes in large part—though not totally—from Judaism. But on the other hand, its essential idea, foreign to Judaism, coincides with that of the mysteries, not because it derives from them but because the spiritual way it proposes corresponds to a universal constant, which, we are going to see, is not limited to the ancient Greco-Oriental world. Besides, if the Holy Fathers adopted the *language* of the mysteries to such an extent—they who 'knew', and knew in particular that it is not foreign to the reality of things—it was clearly because they recognized in these mysteries the universal and fundamental shape of the 'inner' religion.

It is important, we believe, to take a closer look at the parallel between Christianity and the other rites mentioned, not for the pleasure of making 'comparisons', as it is said, with a view to mere information, but because such an examination, by bringing to light a universal pattern of spiritual realization, will enable us to see the extent to which Christianity is rooted in the traditions of humanity and thus answers to the fundamental spiritual exigencies of men of all races. And this without prejudice to Christian Revelation which, far from being weakened by such comparisons, comes away from them strengthened in the eyes of many, which is also, we repeat, one of our principal objectives in writing this book.

We saw above,[5] in what are customarily called the 'mystery religions' (an incorrect term we shall nevertheless keep for convenience sake), centered on a god who suffers, dies, and is resurrected, the faithful gain intimacy with him through the rites he inaugurated, which perpetuate the tradition and ensure salvation. We have outlined the myth, or sacred story, of some of these religions and said very briefly that this story was reproduced in a sort of mystical drama, into which soteriological rites were inserted, a drama in which officiants and faithful participated. It is to this last point that we shall return in our parallel between the non-Christian mysteries

5. See above, p25ff.

and the Christian liturgy. To begin with, we note that the word 'drama', as a way of speaking of these things, is ambiguous and could lead to confusion. We shall nevertheless provisionally keep it by way of a first approach, while what should replace it will be clearer at the end of our analysis.

The ritual of the mysteries includes the following elements as constants: purification, sacrifice and sacred meal, representation of the divine story (what we have called the *memorial*), and communion with the god. What we do not always know exactly, however, is whether a cultural element, among those we are aware of, was reserved solely for initiation ceremonies or was repeated in the regular offices. At this point, this problem is not in fact of great importance, for ultimately we have only the rite of the Mass in view. And we shall see later that the Mass summarizes the whole of Christian initiation and, as a result, includes more or less all the elements of the mystery religions.

To begin with, let us take the ritual of Eleusis. In it we find the mystes' bath of purification, a sacrifice (that of Demeter's piglets), a sacred meal, the 'dramatic' representation of the story of Demeter and Kore, and various rites including the consumption of a sacred drink (the *kykeon*) and the touching of sacred objects (the *hiera*). These last two rites were the symbol of the union of the initiate with the Goddess, which was, on the other hand, guaranteed by the *hierogamos* (sacred marriage) consummated by the pontiff of Eleusis with the priestess, the image of the union of Demeter with Zeus, the supreme god, and condition and pledge of the union of the initiate with the Goddess. After the hierogamos the temple was lit up and the birth of the divine child Brimos announced, the archetype of the initiate who, henceforth, was the 'newborn' (*neophyte*), participating in the divinity.

The oriental mysteries of Attis were as early as the first century of our era compared to the Christian rites by Firmicus Maternus,[6] himself a Christian. Attis was also a slain and resurrected god, like the Eleusinian Kore. The chief ceremony of his cult unfolded at the vernal equinox. After the sacrifice of a bull on the 15th of March, the

---

6. F. Maternus, *De errore...*, 18.

Mourning of the god's death, which took the form of chanting lamentations around a felled pine tree decorated with ribbons, was celebrated on the 22nd. Finally, on the 25th, there was the ceremony of the resurrection of the god, still in the form of a tree. We also know that the initiation, besides a taurobolium and criobolium—playing the role of a baptism—included the consumption of food and a sacred drink, two rites that F. Maternus compared with those of the Last Supper. Finally, there was a rite mysteriously designated by the expression 'slipping beneath the curtains', that is to say, into the nuptial chamber, where the initiate was received as the spouse of Cybele, the Mother.[7] The initiate was symbolically 'killed' with the victim of the sacrifice, the bull, with which he was identified; at the same time he was regenerated by this act and 'reborn' in the womb of the Mother, united with the divinity.

Very similar in their conception to the mysteries of Attis were the Greco-Egyptian mysteries of Isis and Osiris. Their ritual, the aim of which was to enable the initiate to share in the same destiny as Osiris, also a slain and resurrected god, included a commemoration of his passion. Like him, the initiate accomplished a descent into hell, after which he was reborn and ascended towards the light of the sun, appearing as a sort of hypostasis of the latter, which signified that he had acquired immortality.[8]

Tertullian insisted on the resemblance between the Christian rite and that of the Mysteries of Mithras, of Persian origin.[9] The myth recounts how, at the beginning, Mithras killed the divine bull from which all beings emerged; the soul of the bull rose to the gods and became a protecting spirit. Likewise, at the end of time, Saoshyant will kill the same bull, and its fat, mixed with the juice of white *haoma*, will be the elects' drink of immortality. In fact, the bull that

7. This emerges from the formula pronounced by the initiate and transmitted to us by Clement of Alexandria, *Protr.* 2, 15: *ek tympanou ephagon, ek kymbalou epion, ekernophoresa, hypo ton paston hypedyn.* One must needs think that the drum and the cymbal served as plate and cup.

8. On the Egyptian mysteries, the essential texts are Plutarch, *On Isis and Osiris*, and Apuleius, *The Metamorphoses*, Book XI. See our book *La religion égyptienne dans la pensée de Plutarque*, Paris, 1976.

9. Tertullian, *De praescr.* 40; *De Corona*, 15.

Mithras is shown killing with a sword is none other than the god himself. We are faced here with a pattern that should not astonish us: the god at once sacrificer and sacrificed encountered in many a religious domain. In Mithraism, however, the flesh of the bull is not eaten: the sacrifice serves only to baptize the initiate who is sprinkled with the blood of the victim. In the Mithraic banquet, communion with the god is made under the symbol of the bread, which understandably struck Tertullian the Christian. On the other hand, we know through Justin[10] that together with the bread a cup of water was presented. The bread and water were the substitutes for the bull, hence for Mithras. We also know through Justin that formulae of consecration were pronounced over these elements by the 'Father', an initiate of high rank. To conclude, let us add that the water did not have to be pure water, but was certainly mixed with the juice of certain plants to make it a substitute for *haoma*, the drink of immortality, as was done in India for the corresponding *soma*.

True to our promise to show that the ritual pattern we are studying is to be encountered elsewhere than in the mysteries of Greco-Roman antiquity, we shall, by way of concluding this list, say a word about an Aztec rite. This annual rite, reported by a sixteenth century missionary,[11] bore the characteristic name of *Teoqualo*, that is to say 'the eating of the god'. With the crushed and ground seeds of the thorny wild poppy one made a dough from which one fashioned a statuette of the god Uitzilo-pochtli; then the priest, representing Quetzalcoatl, 'killed' the god with a spear; the dough body was cut up and divided among the persons present. We shall shortly see how evocative the Aztec priest's gesture is when we compare it with a certain rite in the Mass, the analysis of which we need to take up again after this detour.

We spoke earlier of the mystical drama, and have seen in the examples just given that, besides the representation of the story of the god, it includes a majority of the other essential rites to be found in the corresponding initiation. The same goes for the Mass. In order, though, to dispel all ambiguity, let us clearly specify how the

---

10. Justin, I *Apol.* 66.
11. *Histoire de Fray Bernardino de Sahagun* (German version of E. Seiler, 1927).

expression 'mystical drama' should be understood. The mistake would be to assimilate this type of representation to the theater, from which it differs radically. To understand this, the Mass should rather be contrasted with the 'Passions' of the fifteenth century performed in front of the cathedrals. The subject is the same in both: the sacrifice of Christ; however, everyone immediately feels there is hardly any connection between these two representations. In short, let us say that the difference depends on two essential causes. First of all, the Mass actually *effects* an objective event, as real as, or even more real than the events of our life. The theatrical piece, on the other hand, is only a *fiction*, which in this case certainly presents an historical event, but as an unavoidably 'illusory' *image*, which moves the imagination and sensibility, but does not act upon the *ontological* plane. These images then, and this point is important, are concrete images of what one wishes to represent, whereas in the Mass there are only *symbols*, because symbols, transcending the sensible, are the only means of *really* and ontologically evoking the invisible. And this is the characteristic mark of all ritual action. Also, to avoid the above mentioned ambiguity, in place of the expression 'mystical drama', it would be preferable to use that of *ritual drama,* or better still, in order to include the symbolic, the expression *ritual mimodrama*, which implies that gestural expression in this case is non-figurative and purely symbolical.[12] And now one more word to finish with these preliminaries. We have just said that symbols are the only adequate channel to convey invisible realities. It is necessary to insist on this point in order to dispel another ambiguity due to the modern mentality. Lately, a certain number of books have appeared, proposing to study the Christian rites in the light of the very fashionable 'human sciences', which, however, only envisage things from the profane point of view of official science. We have already alluded to this in our introduction. There would be nothing astonishing

---

12. We have borrowed the term *mimodrama* from the anthropological works of Fr M. Jousse, who himself has applied it to the Mass. See M. Jousse, *L'Anthropologie du geste*, Paris, 1969, p92. The word is moreover implicitly patristic; thus St Justin, *Mystag. Cat.* 2, 5. (PG 33, 1081) speaking of the ritual of baptism, called it a *mimesis*.

here if the authors of these books, who are clergy, were not also totally imbued with the profane spirit proper to the teaching of such sciences. Furthermore, they think it proper to conduct their research in this spirit, by employing the very special jargon of the 'mandarins' of these sciences, a pseudo-learned jargon, which, while perhaps impressing the vulgar, in every way succeeds in smothering the real problems. Be this as it may, to confine ourselves to the question of symbols, much is said today in the circles we have mentioned about 'symbolical efficacy'. This is so as to 'learnedly' explain to us that among 'primitives', as they say, this efficacy rests upon the belief that the thing symbolized is identical with the symbol, and that in such conditions the symbol can be efficacious by acting on the mind. One immediately sees the danger of such an error when religion is involved. The relationship between symbol and thing symbolized is not of the order of identity, but of analogy, and, regarding this, it is certainly true that the symbol exercises a *psychological* influence. But this is not the cause of its *efficacy*, for that, then, would not transcend the individual domain. The symbol alone does not itself realize the presence of the sacred. For that, it needs to be 'vitalized' by the spiritual influence for which it is, in sum, only the 'vector' to use an image borrowed from physics. We see then the abyss separating ritual reality from profane lucubrations, even when these are the work of clergy.

The sequences in the unfolding of the mimodrama of the Mass are organized in a double structure, according to whether one is considering them from the point of view of the Divine Victim or from that of the officiant and faithful. From the first point of view the Mass is a mimodrama of the life and works of Christ; from the second, it is an integration of Christian initiation in its entirety. It goes without saying, naturally, that these two points of view blend together, if one ceases to consider the *dramatis personae*.

Under this last relationship, the Preparation is a veritable renewal of Christian initiation, or baptism. In the Latin Rite, the sprinkling of water recalls the baptismal water. At any rate, in all the liturgies, the sacred office begins with a renewal, in one form or another, of that initial purification that made a 'saint' of the 'profane' man, that is to say, one 'separated', separated from the impure, this being the indispensable requirement for offering the sacrifice and participating in it.[13] It is the same goal of purification that demands the recitation of the public confession. By avowing sins that have obscured baptismal purity and praying with a view to obtaining pardon, the believer anticipates the Judgment: as has been said, he accuses and 'judges himself' before the divine Majesty and the saints in order 'not to be judged'. The same line of thought is evident again in the recitation of Psalm 42 to be found at this point in a great number of liturgies: 'Judge me, O God, and plead my cause against an ungodly nation: O deliver me from the deceitful and unjust man.' This text evokes the fierce combat against the lower forces the catechumen has to engage with at baptism, the combat against the dragon. The 'unjust man' is fallen man, the egotistical self, in contrast to the *new man*. Now Psalm 42 was, appropriately, sung by the newly baptized, going in procession from the font up to the altar to communicate. We see here good reason to call this part of the Mass the Mass of the catechumens. People have sometimes asked why it continues to be called this, since there are now hardly any catechumens to dismiss before the eucharistic sacrifice. This, precisely, is to misunderstand one of the aims of the Holy Liturgy, which periodically permits the Christian to renew in a way his baptismal initiation and relive it. After all, the sequence of the Preparation follows the latter's stages. After the exorcisms, the catechumens 'received' the Evangelistary, the Creed and the Lord's Prayer. At the vigil of the final initiation of baptism proper, they had to 'repeat the symbol' (the Creed), that is to say recite it publicly as profession of their faith. From there to the Mass, there followed the readings from the Epistles and the Gospel, and the solemn chanting of the Creed. This repetition in the Preparation of the step by step approach of the catechumens is all the more necessary today since baptism is administered to the newly-born who can have no recollection of the rite of initiation, which has such a profound effect upon the adult. Beyond the offertory, the believer recapitulates the other two stages of his complete initiation: the reception of the Holy Spirit and communion in the body of

---

13. A confession before offering the sacrifice was required in the Old Testament: Lev. 1–4, 2 Ezra 9:2.

Christ. The descent of the Spirit is linked to several rites, which we shall study, just as communion is signified in advance by a certain number of others, which mark out the sacrificial mimodrama. Thus, from the point of view of mystical theology, this mimodrama is a synthesis of the three stages of the 'way': the purgative life, the illuminative life, and the unitive life.

From the Holy Victim's point of view, the mimodrama again unfolds according to two different structures. The first is what could be called the structure of sacrifice with its three essential acts: offering, immolation, and communion. It is inscribed in a greater, second one, the one evoking symbolically the principal facts of the Saviour's life before and after His sacrifice and constituting the representation of the whole of that 'mystery of salvation' about which we have spoken. In fact, these two structures interlace and interlock in such a way that it is hardly possible to separate them by analysis, but they need to be borne in mind if the composition of the mimodrama is to be understood properly. Notice also that certain of the events mentioned are not in their historical chronological order, which is often confusing. This need not surprise us for, as we said, the time of the *ritual remembrance* is not ordinary time, but a time outside time, so to say, or rather, an eternal instant. In that case, then, all the events being simultaneous, there is no need to establish a chronological order. As a result the mimodrama sometimes presents them by anticipation, even repeating an event in two forms, according to an order determined by pedagogic intent, or rather by that 'mystagogical catechesis' forming the mimodrama of the liturgy.

Finally, the two structures in question are dominated by the two great symbols of Bread and Wine, which synthesize all their elements. So we shall begin our analysis with them.

These two symbols, being the principal foods that sustain natural life for a large part of humanity, are certainly the most adequate to the very object of the Holy Sacrifice, the source of spiritual life. Besides, their symbolism functions at several levels, thereby constituting a marvelous propaedeutic of the eucharistic mystery. Thus, from the beginning of Christianity, the bread and wine of the altar were seen as a sign of unity, a recapitulation of the multiple in unity. The following lines come from the eucharistic anaphora preserved in a text called the *Didache*, the 'Teaching of the Apostles':

> As this broken bread, once scattered on the mountains [when it was only grains of wheat], was gathered to make but one, gather likewise Thy Church from the ends of the earth into Thy Kingdom.

Similarly, as the wine has flowed from many grapes into a single cup, so the faithful also need to become one in Christ. These images have passed into the Syrian anaphoras. What is more, the cultivation of wheat and the making of wine and bread are striking images of sacrifice and spiritual rebirth. The ears of wheat 'scattered on the mountains' have sprung from the seed buried in the earth: 'If the seed die not,' said Jesus (John 12:24), who was Himself placed in the earth, dead, then raised while multiplying Himself in the faithful raised with Him. This is the mystery of death and resurrection. Likewise, in order to become bread and wine, the wheat and grapes have undergone a sort of 'passion': the grain has been ground, the grapes pressed, but both, after this 'death', are 'brought to life' again in a more noble form, bread and wine. To this symbolism inscribed in nature itself, let us add, regarding the bread, a particularly remarkable meaning included in Scripture. 'Bread' and 'flesh', in Hebrew, are expressed by the same root *lhm,* which in the word *lihum* signifies 'flesh' and vocalized *lehem,* 'bread'. We see in this the narrowness of the linguistic bond and the sort of wordplay in the words of Christ: 'This [the bread] is my body [flesh].' Finally, let us remember the extraordinary interconnection constituted by the birth of Christ at Bethlehem, that is to say the 'House of Bread', and His being defined as 'the living bread descended from heaven', the descent being effectively realized at Bethlehem.

Wine symbolism is so rich and extensive that one would need an entire volume simply to review all its aspects. We shall merely recall the essentials.[14]

In Christianity, wine plays the role of the draught of immortality, which, in other traditions, has been filled by various drinks, either pure water (obviously sacralized) or a mixture of different plant

---

14. Cf. K Kericher, *Die sakrale Bedeutung des Weines in Altertum.*

juices as we saw above regarding *soma*. It is primarily its resemblance to blood that has led to its being chosen for this function; wine is 'the blood of the grape', we read in Deuteronomy (32:14). And blood being the support of the 'soul of life', as proclaimed by Scripture (Deut. 12:23, Lev. 17:11–14), it was naturally designated to be the image of the Divine Blood—the principle of the higher spiritual life—which Christ orders us to drink under the species of wine. Jesus is Himself called the Vine (John 15:1), and it is this passage in the Gospel that inspired the following magnificent verse from a Byzantine hymn: 'O Christ, like a vine attached to the wood [of the Cross], Thou hast sprinkled the earth with the wine of immortality.'[15] From this context of ideas and images the famous theme of the Mystical Winepress emerged in the West in the fifteenth century. On the central panel of Jean Bellegambe's triptych, 'The Mystical Bath', we see the cross planted in the middle of a vat; blood gushes from the side of Christ and flows into the vat, where men bathe themselves. Sometimes the symbolism is more pronounced, the vertical branch of the cross becoming the screw of a press. An ancient sequence of Adam of St Victor translates the violent beauty of this theme of the bath of blood: 'Under the sacred press of the cross, the grapes overflow into the bosom of the well-beloved Church; expressed with force, the wine flows, its sweetness plunging the first fruit of the Gentile nations into a joyful drunkenness.'[16] Every contemplative has hymned this mystical drunkenness, provoked by the spiritual wine, from Solomon in the *Song of Songs* (1:6–14), through St Bernard,[17] to St John of the Cross.[18] The physiological effects of wine, which abolish the everyday condition and afford euphoria, explain how it can symbolize the spiritual operation whereby man is snatched from his limited, individual condition, emerges from

---

15. Triodion of Friday, first week of Lent.

16. See our book, *Divine Craftsmanship* p95ff. Add the famous window in the Parisian Church of Saint-Etienne-du-Mont.

17. *Treatise on the Love of God*, 11, 32. Cf., *Sermons on the Song of Solomon*, passim.

18. *Spiritual Canticle*, verse 17. We find the same theme of wine and mystical drunkenness with a Muslim contemplative, the Sufi Umar ibn-al-Fārīd, *In Praise of Wine* (*Al-Khamriya*).

himself and is assumed into the divine Personality. And this is properly the aim—we shall return to this—of the communion of the Flesh and Blood of the Saviour. Regarding this, the blood is the symbol of the Great Eucharistic mystery under its two aspects: transubstantiation of the gifts and metamorphosis of the believer, which, to the well-informed, is indicated by the 'identity' of the two Hebrew words: *yain*, 'wine', and *sod*, 'mystery', which have gematrically the same number: 70.[19]

One word, to end this small excursus, on the symbolism of the chalice, or the 'cup of salvation'. Here again, there are a multiplicity of meanings. We shall mention only one, the most important for understanding the sacrifice of the Mass. With this one the cup is recognized to be a symbol of the heart, because every vessel, moreover, symbolizes the heart which is a 'vessel of blood'. What is more, in several traditions, both are represented by one and the same shape, that of an inverted triangle.

If this figure is prolonged with a vertical line, starting from the lowest point, we immediately see the perfect figure of a cup or glass with a foot. Thus the symbolism of the chalice completes that of the wine: it represents the Heart of Christ filled with His Blood.[20]

---

19. Gematria is an auxiliary traditional science, which aims at interpreting the meaning of a word through the numerical value of the letters composing it. It goes without saying that such an operation is only possible in those languages such as Hebrew, Arabic, Greek, or Sanskrit, in which each letter has a numerical value.

20. It would be interesting to talk here of the Grail, the cup which, according to legend, Christ used at the Last Supper and in which Joseph of Arimathea collected the blood flowing from His wounds after His death. The latter took it to Britain, but it was lost. The search for it occasioned the exploits of the mystical knights,

If the first part of the Mass, or Preparation, is more especially an office of praise and instruction, its difference in relation to the central part should not be exaggerated. The ritual mimodrama is a homogeneous whole forming a harmonious ensemble representing, we repeat, the complete mystery of salvation. Nicholas Cabasilas writes:

> The whole scheme of Christ's work . . . is depicted in the Host during the liturgy; there we see the symbol of the infant Christ, of Christ led to death, crucified, and pierced with a lance; then we see the bread transformed into the most holy Body which actually endured these sufferings, and rose from the dead, and ascended into Heaven, where it sits at the right hand of the Father.[21]

Broadly speaking, the Liturgy of the Catechumens refers to Christ's life on earth, and that of the Faithful to His death, resurrection and ascension.

While this symbolic representation is most developed and apparent in the Byzantine Mass and the Oriental liturgies in general, we shall see that its essentials are nevertheless to be found in the Roman Mass. In the Byzantine Mass, the preparation of the Holy Gifts has assumed a particular importance, which we shall dwell upon in a moment in connection with the offertory, given their very close connection. However, it is a symbolism of this first rite that needs to be mentioned right away, because it inaugurates the representation of Christ's earthly life. According to Cabasilas,[22] the gifts in the first stage of the Mass represent the body of the Lord at the beginning of

---

principally Perceval (Wagner's *Parsifal*). The correspondences of the Grail with the Eucharist are obvious. But the question raises too many problems to attempt even to simply outline it here. Finally, recall that the Eucharistic chalice is not unconnected with the hermetic vessel (we are speaking naturally of orthodox spiritual hermeticism). On the other hand the correspondences some would see between the procession of the Grail described in the mediaeval romances and the Byzantine liturgy are extremely doubtful.

21. N. Cabasilas, *A Commentary on the Divine Liturgy*, Chap. 37.
22. Ibid., Chap. 11.

His life, for they have not yet been consecrated. After preparing them in the way we shall describe, the priest places them on the paten, covering them with asterisk and veil. The asterisk is a cross, equipped with a foot and vertical screw, from which a small star, whence its name (*astiriskon* in Greek), is suspended. When placing the asterisk, the priest pronounces the words from St Matthew 2:9: 'The star came and stood over where the young child was.' The paten, moreover, is assimilated to the crèche, and the altar of the prothesis to the cave of the nativity. Finally, the priest covers everything with a cloth, because, Cabasilas further tells us, the divine power was hidden before the time of the manifestation of Jesus. The latter takes place symbolically at the moment of the Small Entrance, that is to say the Gospel procession. The officiant after the singing of the anthems proceeds to the showing of the Evangelistary; facing the faithful, he lifts the book on high and this gesture signifies the manifestation of the Saviour, His starting to disclose Himself to the crowds. The same thing is suggested, albeit much less obviously, by the small procession of the Gospel in the Roman Mass.

With the offertory we enter into the structure of the sacrifice properly so-called, a fundamental and indispensable element of which it is. In antiquity the offertory assumed a breadth and solemnity we no longer understand today, at least in the West. It was during the course of the Mass after the Gospel that both at Rome and in Gaul, the faithful brought their offerings of loaves and wine etc., from which what was needed for the sacrifice was taken. In the East, the offerings were brought before the Mass. The part set aside for the consecration was solemnly carried to the altar, as we read in Denis the Areopagite.[23] The rite's essentials are preserved in the Great Entrance of the Byzantine rite. The officiant and the deacon, preceded by acolytes with candles and thurifer, leave the sanctuary with the gifts and traverse the nave of the church before returning to the altar, thus symbolizing the triumphal procession of the universal king accompanied by angels.

One cannot over-exaggerate the importance of the offertory in the ritual of the sacrifice, contrary to the attitude of certain Western

23. *The Ecclesiastical Hierarchy,* 3, 2.

liturgists who see in the offertory nothing but a simple preparation of the gifts. Doubtless it will be said that in the beginning the offering was made in silence, being simply the physical placing of the gifts on the altar, and that the present offertory is only an anticipation of the anaphora, or canon, which is the true moment of the offering. This, however, is an unacceptable point of view. First, the history of religions reminds us that the phase of the offering in the sacrifice is everywhere extremely ritualized and accompanied with appropriate words and gestures. Thus, in ancient Egypt, there were the two very distinct moments of the 'deposition' (*wah*) of the offering on the altar and its 'elevation' (*fay*). What is more, the offering of the offertory is not exactly that of the canon: in the first instance, it is that of the faithful, while in the second, it is that of Christ through the intermediary of the priest. Moreover, to say that the actual offertory anticipates the canon is not untrue. And this is quite normal; the mimodrama of the sacrifice, we have said, is homogeneous, for the sacrifice more or less directly governs all its elements. The offertory is already, and necessarily, a sacrificial act. This is why in all liturgies of both East and West we find the same phenomenon of anticipation—if we still want to retain this word— of the anaphora. This is very clear not only in the Roman Mass,[24] but in other liturgies, like the Coptic and Ethiopian:

> Make this offering agreeable in Thy sight, O Lord; make us worthy to offer it to Thee in expiation for our sins and the faults of Thy people; may it be sanctified through the operation of the Holy Spirit, etc. (Coptic Mass). May this host attract to Thy people the pardon and remission of their sins (Ethiopian Mass).

In these two cases, one sees that the gifts are treated in advance as if they had already been consecrated, in the same way as in the Roman Mass. It is in the Byzantine liturgy, however, that the sacrificial and propitiatory character has seen the greatest development. We have already seen the breadth assumed by the procession of the gifts; this procession was, however, originally preceded by their preparation.

24. We are speaking of the old Roman rite, for in the new, the offertory is so meager one wonders if it still exists.

Actually, this preparation (*proskomede*) has been placed at the beginning of the office where it was enlarged to take on the dimensions of a complete small mimodrama within the mimodrama as a whole and constitutes a striking parallel with the Aztec rite of the *Teoqualo* mentioned above. Five loaves are placed on the small altar called the *prothesis*, situated to the left of the main altar. From the first one, the priest removes a central piece marked with a cross and the following letters:

IC	XP
NI	KA

which is to say: *Iesous Christos nika* (Jesus Christ Victor). This piece of bread is called the 'lamb', a very significant designation. The priest takes a small spear and buries it in the right side while saying: 'Like a sheep, he was led to the slaughter'; and then in the left side while saying: 'and as a spotless lamb is dumb before the shearer, so He opened not His mouth.' Thereafter he sinks the spear above the imprint of the letters, then aslant to the right, lifts the holy lamb and places it upside down on the disk (paten). Then, he 'immolates' (*thyi*) the lamb by scoring it deeply in the form of a cross while saying: 'He is immolated (*thyete*), the Lamb of God who takes away the sin of the world, for the life of the world and its salvation.' Then he turns it over, so that the mark of the cross is above and pierces the Lamb on the right side while saying: 'One of the soldiers pierced his side with the lance and immediately blood and water came forth from it.' After which, he pours the wine and the water into the chalice. One clearly sees that, as Cabasilas says, 'everything done then is like an enacted account of the sufferings and death, the causes of our salvation.'[25] The purpose of the sequel to this mimodrama is to highlight the union of the whole Church with the sacrifice of Its Head. From the second of the five loaves the priest removes a portion in honor of Mary; from the third, 9 pieces in honor of 9 saints;

---

25. Cabasilas, op. cit., 6 and 8.

from the fourth an indefinite number of pieces for the living who are to be remembered and finally, from the fifth, pieces for the dead. All these pieces are arranged on the disk, which is carried to the altar and placed to the left of the chalice. The pieces from the first three loaves form the first row with the lamb in the middle; the others are below in two parallel rows (see ill.). Long ago the West knew a similar arrangement of the gifts. At Monte Cassino in the twelfth century, the hosts were placed in the form of a cross on the disk. In eleventh-century Spain, five loaves were placed in the form of a cross; while, at Christmas, five of the seventeen loaves were in the form of a cross (see ill.).

In all Masses, of both East and West, the offertory includes a very important rite that was referred to above, the mixing of water with the wine in the chalice. This rite is clearly inspired by the Gospel of St John and represents one or two events in this Gospel. If one refers to the Eastern liturgies one must needs think of the Transfixion of Christ on Golgotha. Thus, in the Syrian liturgy during the mixing the officiant says: 'With a spear one of the soldiers pierced his side, and forthwith came there out blood and water. And he that saw it bare record, and his record is true' (John 19:33–36). The remembrance of this fact is especially significant in as much as the cup of the chalice symbolizes the heart. The transfixion and the flow of water and blood is a capital theme with St John who returns to it in an epistle:

This is he that came by water and blood, even Jesus Christ; not by water only, but by water and blood. And it is the Spirit that beareth witness, because the Spirit is truth... there are three that bear witness on earth, the Spirit, and the water and the blood: and these three agree in one (1 John 5:6–8).

The Latin rite has a different prayer.

O God, who hast established the nature of man in wondrous dignity and even more wondrously hast renewed it, grant that through the mystery of this water and wine, we may be made partakers of His divinity, who has deigned to become partaker of our humanity, Jesus Christ, thy Son, our Lord, etc.

This prayer implicitly relates the mixing to the miracle of the Marriage at Cana. This miracle, recounted only by St John, was Christ's first miracle, to which the Christian tradition quite rightly attaches an exceptional importance, for it foreshadows the whole of Jesus' teaching life and the goal itself of His teaching and earthly manifestation. This transmutation of the water into wine is the token of our regeneration. It is the reintegration of purified Nature (the water) into the intoxicating way of spiritual Life (the wine), of fallen Adam into a way implying for him the possibility of becoming a 'son of God'. On the other hand, the miracle at Cana is like the preface of the Last Supper where the second phase of the mystery was accomplished: the wine (and the water mixed with it) became the Divine Blood, the vehicle of the Divine Life, in the Spiritual Vine. This second interpretation of the rite does not exclude the first, quite the contrary, for the two facts are linked. One can even relate the water (as grace purifying nature) and the blood (expiation and revivification) to the double regeneration, the necessity of which Christ affirmed to Nicodemus: 'Except a man be born of water and of the Spirit, he cannot enter into the kingdom of God' (John 3:5), since the Divine Blood is the vehicle of the Life-giving Spirit.

It should be carefully noted that the thought of the immolation of Christ, which will only be ritually realized at the Consecration, permeates every stage of the offertory. In the Syrian rite, the death of Christ is commemorated in every part of the Mass, from the procession of the gifts to the epiclesis. The procession depicts Christ going to His passion; the placing of the gifts on the altar, the committing of the victim to immolation and, above all, the committing to the tomb. Moreover, the silken cloth upon which the gifts are placed, called the *antimension*, bears a representation of the laying-out of the Saviour. The fine-linen cloth of the Latins, the corporal, plays the same role and is assimilated to the shroud. Still with the Syrian rite, the gifts placed on the antimension are covered with a cloth, which is assimilated to the stone rolled across the entrance of the sepulchre. When the priest simultaneously lifts and shakes it, after the consecration and before the epiclesis, he pronounces these words: 'You are the hard rock that was placed before the tomb of Our Lord.'

In the Latin rite, just before the recital of the institution, the priest extends his hand over the gifts while pronouncing a prayer which leaves no doubt as to the meaning of this gesture. It is familiar to us, being the ancient gesture of the *semikha*, mentioned earlier, signifying the transfer from him who offers to him who is offered, the transfer whereby simultaneously the offerer is designated as the gift he offers and unburdens his sins upon the latter. The consecration of the gifts is naturally the climax of the liturgical mimodrama. After giving thanks to God at the beginning of the anaphora and recalling, at least summarily in anaphoras that have remained faithful to their beginnings,[26] the stages of human and salvation history, the officiant arrives at the end of this history—which is none other than the mystery of Christ—at the passion of Christ, at his sacrifice, and at the institution of the Eucharist. The recounting of the institution is the heart and summit of the ritual mimodrama, which it dominates with its majestic simplicity and suprahuman grandeur. Apart from some details, the text of the recital is the same, for obvious reasons, in all the liturgies: nothing of the words that effect the sacrifice should be changed. We shall give the text of the Roman Mass, it being without doubt the most complete.

Who, the day before He suffered, took bread into His holy and venerable hands, and having raised His eyes to heaven, unto Thee, O God, His Father almighty, giving thanks to Thee, blessed, broke it, and gave it to His disciples, saying: 'Take ye all and eat of this: for this is my body.' In like manner, when the supper was done, taking also this goodly chalice into His holy and venerable hands, again giving thanks to Thee, He blessed it and gave it to His disciples, saying: 'Take ye all, and drink of this: for this is the chalice of my blood of the new and eternal covenant: the mystery of faith, which shall be shed for you and for many unto the forgiveness of sins.'

26. There are very few. Only the anaphora of St Basil (cf. above, p 42 ff) still contains a recapitulation of the history of salvation. The old Roman canon totally abandoned this recapitulation except for a few bits reintroduced in the Prefaces. It is true, the fourth anaphora in the new Roman ritual recovers some of its old formulae, but unfortunately, it is almost never used.

We are faced here with the perfect type of *ritual remembrance*; the qualified person, the priest, solemnly reads the sacred account telling of the Divine act that is to be actualized in the rite; at the same time the priest, identifying himself with the god himself, re-enacts the gestures and re-pronounces exactly the divine words. This is the universal way of operating.[27] The Christian priest, then, as he reads the text, reproduces in gestures the primordial operation of Christ. When reading: 'He took the bread in His hands', he himself takes the Host in his hands; 'lifting His eyes heavenward to Thee, O God': he casts his eyes upwards; 'He blessed it': he blesses the host with the sign of the cross; after which he solemnly pronounces the words of consecration. We say solemnly, because normally the consecration is made aloud, according to a particular rhythmomelody, which in the oriental rites underlines its sacred character. This is above all the case in the Syrian, Maronite, and Assyro-Chaldean rites, where, the liturgical language being Aramaic, one hears the holy words proclaimed in the very language in which they were pronounced *in illo tempore*. The same scenario is repeated, naturally, for the consecration of the chalice.

In this central rite of consecration there is reason to distinguish two occurrences: transubstantiation and immolation. The gifts, the bread and wine, change nature and are transformed into the body and blood of Christ. On the other hand the consecration is done twice and separately for the bread and the wine, and it is these two separate consecrations that constitute the immolation of the victim, whose blood, the vehicle of life, is drained from its body. For the Latins, the rite ends there.[28] In the East, the recital of the institution

27. Thus, among the Karok, Hirpa, and Yurok (California), at the time of the New Year ceremony, called 'The Repair of the World', the priest undertakes long pilgrimages to the sacred sites and during this period incarnates the Immortals. M. Eliade, *Myth and Reality*, p41 ff. In Africa, among the Dogons, the priest of the Nommo is completely identified with the latter in the rites. M. Griaule, *Dieu d'eau*, p114. In ancient Egypt, at the Feast of Enthronement of the king, the two priests were assimilated to the gods Horus and Seth for the purposes of investing him with dominion over the country. Likewise, in the funerary rites and those of Isism the priest was assimilated to the god Anubis. In both cases, the assimilation was underlined by the fact that the priests wore the mask of the god they were incarnating.

28. In the new Roman order, an epiclesis has been reintroduced, but placed before the recital of the institution.

is followed by the epiclesis, that is, the invocation of the Holy Spirit. In the Syrian Mass, for example—but things happen in nearly the same way in the other Masses—the celebrant shakes his hands above the gifts, miming the descent of the Spirit, while the deacon says: 'How terrible this hour and redoubtable this moment, but most precious, when the Holy Spirit comes from sublime celestial spheres, descends upon this Eucharist and consecrates it. Stand aright and pray in silence and awe.' Then the priest pronounces the epiclesis: 'We prostrate before Thee and beseech Thee, Almighty Lord and God of the Heavenly Powers to send Thy Holy Spirit upon us and upon the gifts before us and make this bread the venerable body of Our Lord Jesus Christ, and this chalice, the blood of this same Jesus Christ, Our Lord.' This appeal to the Holy Spirit, the Spirit of fire, is naturally the Christian version of the heavenly fire falling upon the sacrifice under the Old Law, for example at the time of the sacrifice offered by Elijah (1 Kings 18:36, 37, 38. Cf. Ezek. 37:9): 'Hear me, O Lord, hear me. Then the fire of the Lord fell, and consumed the burnt sacrifice.' These words of Elijah are included in the epiclesis of the Maronite mass.

Before the communion, other significant rites take place, the principal being the breaking of the bread and the mixing together of the Holy Species, to be found in all Eastern and Western liturgies.

Because it is of Divine institution, the breaking of the bread is an absolutely essential rite, so much so that in the first centuries the expression 'breaking of bread' often served to designate the celebration of the Eucharist. It can be done in different ways; in the Roman rite, the priest divides the host into three pieces. In the Byzantine rite, he breaks the Holy Bread into four pieces, which he arranges on the disk in the form of a cross:

IC

NI   KA

XC

while saying: 'He is broken and shared, the Lamb of God, the son of the Father, broken but not divided, everywhere eaten, and nowhere consumed, but who sanctifies those who partake of Him.' These words clearly indicate the symbolic meaning of the action of breaking; it is a *mimesis* of the violent death of Christ, in conformity with His Word: 'Take and eat all of it: This is my Body which will be broken and given for you and for many for the remission of sins and life eternal' (consecration of the bread in the Syrian Mass). 'Take, eat; this is my Body which is broken for you, for the remission of sins' (consecration in the Byzantine Mass).

After breaking the sacred Bread, the priest places a piece in the chalice, in such a way that it is mixed with the wine. This is the commixing. This rite is a *mimesis* of the resurrection: the body is reunited with the soul, symbolized especially by the blood, as we have already said.[29] In the Assyro-Chaldean rite, after the commixing, the priest removes the cloth that has been wrapped around the chalice since the beginning of the eucharistic sacrifice; this cloth is called 'Golgotha' because it symbolizes both the sepulchre and the stone of the sepulchre. It is removed after the commixing because the resurrection has then taken place.

We would like to respond here to certain liturgists who contest the soundness of this symbolism of the breaking and mixing. At the beginning, according to them, these two rites would have been only utilitarian acts of some kind or other: one broke the bread to distribute it and mixed a piece of the host consecrated the day before, or at the bishop's Mass, with the Holy Blood to mark (which in itself was somewhat symbolical) the continuity of the eucharistic sacrifice. The symbolism of the death and resurrection would have been added subsequently and would have had only a secondary importance. Such reasoning, based as always on a purely historical and genetic conception, is in reality worthless. Supposing things were at the beginning as these liturgists claim—which is far from proven, given that the symbolism of which we speak appeared very early in the liturgies and liturgical commentaries throughout both East and West—the fact still remains that the symbolism in question would not have been added artificially. In fact, it needs to be remembered that every image, like every action, can assume several

---

29. Already a very old symbolism, for the West, with Amalaire, *De eccles. off.* 31.

meanings by its very nature, without all these meanings necessarily appearing at the same time. Besides, if the image or action, which is itself a sort of image, are integral to a whole, it is important not to treat them in isolation. The whole constitutes a global structure, all of whose parts and elements are dependent upon and interact with each other; and it is the dominant element, or elements, of the structure that determine and orient the symbolism of the different images. Thus in the case in point, it is evident that the actions of breaking bread and mixing it with a liquid necessarily comprise, among their possible significations, the most general, to wit: every act of breaking an object and every act of reuniting two objects. On the other hand, the dominant element of the mimodrama being the representation of the mystery of Christ under the species of bread and wine become His flesh and His blood, it necessarily follows that the breaking of the host signifies *also* and, we say, even fundamentally, the breaking of His body, and that the mixing of the host, that is to say His body, with the wine, which is His blood, necessarily signifies the reunion of His soul (the blood) with His body, and therefore the resuscitation of the being. It is of little importance, therefore, that the symbolism was perhaps not immediately perceived; it is not, for all that, less inherent in the actions themselves included within the global structure. If we have insisted somewhat upon this point, it is because the problem is posed, and will be again, on many occasions for other cases of symbols, in connection with which the same people have often made the same objections. We shall see some examples of this immediately.

After the consecration in the Armenian Mass, the priest lifts the Holy Species while saying that in this way he commemorates the Ascension of the Saviour; then he bears them lightly to his left while saying that in this way he recalls the Sitting of the Son on the right hand of the Father. In the Roman rite, the Ascension is commemorated, according to the liturgists, by the prayer *Supplices te rogamus*: 'Most humbly we implore Thee, almighty God, bid these our mystic offerings to be brought by the hands of Thy holy Angel unto Thy altar above, before the face of Thy divine majesty. . . .' (cf. Apoc. 5:6, 8:3–4).

Before communion, the Byzantine liturgy practises a rite that is not to be found elsewhere: the *zeon*. This Greek word, meaning 'boiling', designates the hot water the priest pours in the form of a cross into the chalice with the words: 'The ardor of Faith, full of the Holy Spirit.' This action commemorates the descent of the Spirit through Christ upon the Church after the conclusion of the redemptive work, seeing that the sacrifice is accomplished.[30]

And, in fact, the rites we have just described commemorate, by word and action, all the stages of the mystery of salvation. If the consecration of the Holy Species realizes the immolation of the victim, the rites that follow recall the resurrection, the ascension, the sitting on the right hand of the Father, as was proclaimed in the prayer of the anaphora itself,[31] and, finally, the pouring out of the Holy Spirit, which seals the economy of salvation. Thus the God who is going to give Himself in communion, is not a dead but a living god, or more exactly, a god at once dead and alive, immolated and revived. We have here the essentials of sacrifice, as we have defined it, *death and resurrection*, passage through death in order to enter the divine world in the footsteps of the god.[32]

This last stage of the sacrifice is the communion. One has seen how sharing in the offering through eating it, or a part of it, is encountered in a great number of sacrifices: 'eating the god' in order to live again with him, from his life, such is the object of the sacrifice.

'Unless you eat My flesh, and drink My blood, you will have no life in you.' For our participation in His sacrifice, Christ could not have found a support better adapted than this, which has come from the depths of the ages and is common to all humanity. Food is the most adequate symbol to represent the mystery of participation, of communion in the divine, for, in itself, food is already a mystery. To feed one's self is not simply a physiological, but a religious act, because one eats the creations of God. Moreover, each meal puts man in relation with creative forces issuing from the eternal life of the Divinity. This sentiment, to such a degree obliterated in the modern world that has lost the religious meaning of organic functions, is still alive among certain peoples called 'savages'. Thus the

---

30. See Cabasilas, op. cit.
31. See above, p 45, and all the anaphoras after the Consecration.
32. See above, p 23 ff, cf. p 18.

Kanaks of New Caledonia always eat in silence and are scandalized by the attitude of Europeans who chatter during meals. Food for them is still the living receptacle of the nourishing powers of the sun and should be eaten in silence with an attentive mind and heart.[33] By way of food, then, man participates in a higher reality: he eats something that is precious, because it comes from God, and in doing so shares in a mystery, that of the renewal of his body through the foods that are transubstantiated into his flesh.

In the sacrificial meal, however, the symbolism of nourishment and its operation undergoes a radical change. There, in effect, the food, having been consecrated, is charged with a much higher power than that at the origin of food in general, and in the case of the Eucharist, is even identified entirely with the Divinity. Thus the relations between man and this food are no longer those of ordinary meals. By virtue of the law that the greater necessarily prevails over the lesser, the consecrated food prevails over him who absorbs it. Doubtless, man starts by 'eating the god', but immediately, by a total reversal, it is so to say 'the god who eats the man'. St Augustine saw and expressed this clearly. In the Eucharist, man is assumed by Christ, Bread and Wine, and incorporated into Him, such that, in the words of the Apostle, 'It is no longer I who live, but Christ who lives in me.'

This intimate union of the soul with God in the Eucharist is also expressed by images of a different kind, belonging to nuptial symbolism. The Eucharist is not simply a sacrificial meal; it is also a wedding feast. The nuptial symbolism in Christianity is too well known and vast for us to think of going into it in detail here, which would, moreover, be to stray beyond the bounds of this chapter. In order to throw light on this aspect of the Eucharist, we shall content ourselves with recalling its essential traits.

From the beginning the conjugal union has been taken as a symbol of the union of Christ with the Church, presented respectively as Groom and Bride. The most explicit scriptural passages in this regard are those of the *Epistle to the Ephesians* and the *Apocalypse*.

---

33. Leenhardt, *Gens de la Grande-Terre*, cited by Van der Leeuw, *La religion comme essence et manifestation*, p349.

Christ loved the Church, says St Paul, as husband loves wife. A husband loves his wife as his own body and 'he who loves his wife, loves himself.' We are members of the Body of Christ and at this point he recalls the words from Gen. 2:24: 'Therefore shall a man leave his father and his mother, and shall cleave unto his wife: and they shall be one flesh.' 'This is a great mystery: but I speak concerning Christ and the church' (Eph. 5:25–32), adds St Paul. And elsewhere, to the Corinthians, he says: 'for I have espoused you to one husband, that I may present you as a chaste virgin to Christ (2 Cor. 11:2). Likewise in the *Apocalypse*, especially in the last chapters, there is only talk of the 'Nuptials of the Lamb' in the Heavenly Jerusalem, who is His bride (Apoc. 19:8, 21:2 and 9, 22:17). And the elect are invited to this 'marriage supper of the Lamb' (Apoc. 19:9), a feast of immortality where the Lamb Himself is given as food to the elect. One perceives here the meeting point between nuptial and nutritional symbolism, two symbolisms whose closeness is well known to psychology and anthropology. Let us add that, in Christianity, nuptial symbolism is an inheritance from the Jews, among whom the community of Israel has often been assimilated to the Bride of the Eternal. This theme received a magnificent development in the *Song of Songs*, whence it was transmitted to the whole race of mystics, for whom it is no longer solely the 'community' of the faithful, but the soul of each one of them that is the bride of the Divinity. But it is not so much this reference to Judaism that will engage us, for we are less concerned here with biblical than with universal typology. What interests us is observing that the use of nuptial symbols in a sacred mystery, a mimodrama like the Mass, is, like that of the symbols of nutrition, a practice belonging to the very depths of man and to the sacred universally. In both cases, it is a question of the awareness of the sacredness of physiological functions.

With love, however, we obviously find ourselves at a much higher level. In human love, if sufficiently intense, we easily discover a metaphysical basis in one of its characteristics, which is transcendence: transcendence with regard to the individual being. Love is one of those things that transport the individual out of him or herself, that displace the center of the self beyond the self. It is one of the ways whereby a door to the instinct of the individual to surpass his limits opens. In fact, in love man comes into contact with creative Divine Energy and one can say that love is a prolonging of the creative act.[34] All of this is well known in traditional societies where marriage is assimilated to a sacred mystery. In ancient Greece, for example, marriage (*gamos*) unfolded according to a ritual closely related to that of initiation, the name of which: *telos, telia*, it sometimes bore. Moreover, during its course the same formula was pronounced: 'I have escaped from the bad, I have found the good,'[35] which conveys the awareness of the beginning of a new life containing a new power. In India, the conjugal act is expressly thought of as that prolongation of creation spoken of a moment ago. The husband is assimilated to *Purusha*, the creative principle, and the wife to *Prakriti*, or Universal Nature, the creation of the universe being the product of the union of the Divinity with Universal Nature.[36] The same point of view explains the already mentioned hierogamies of the ancient Mysteries,[37] which serve as a support for the representation of union with the divinity.

Such is the context within which the nuptial symbolism of the Eucharist is inscribed, a symbolism which, as we have seen, is expressly linked by St Paul to the marriage of the spouses. For if man and wife according to Genesis 'are but one flesh', 'he that is joined unto the Lord [in communion] is one spirit' (1 Cor. 6:15–17). The union of the spouses is sealed with a kiss, and the latter occupies a very important place in the mimodrama of the Mass. To keep to the essential, we shall only recall the most characteristic, the kiss to the altar. One knows that the altar, about which we shall soon speak, is assimilated to Christ Himself; the kiss to the altar is therefore a kiss

34. Cf. Muhyiddin Ibn-Arabi, *Fusus al-hikam*: 'The conjugal act corresponds to the projection of the Divine Will over that which, at the very moment He creates it, He creates in His form so to recognize Himself there.' Woman is 'like Universal Nature (*at-tabi'ah*) in relation to God. It is within Universal Nature that God discloses the forms of the world through the projection of His Will and through the Divine Act, which is manifested as sexual act in the world of forms constituted by the elements, and as spiritual will in the world of the spirits of light....'

35. *Éphygon kakòn, hèvron àminon.*

36. This is an analogous conception to that of Ibn-Arabi, note 34 above.

37. Cf. above, pp 52–53.

given to Christ. It is the kiss of the Bride to the Divine Groom, through the intermediary of the priest who represents the assembly of the faithful. In the Roman rite the priest kisses the altar as many as eight times in the course of the Mass; in particular before turning to the faithful to greet them with the *Dominus vobiscum*. One sees the highly suggestive meaning of this gesture: through the kiss, which symbolically reiterates the union with Christ, the priest receives power from On-High, and turning towards the faithful with hands extended, pours grace upon them. The priest 'takes' Christ through the kiss and transmits Him to the people: 'The Lord be with you', with you in the nuptial union He desires. This is not a simple salutation, but a transmission of grace.

The same applies to the kiss of peace before communion. The priest kisses the altar and through the deacon, transmits the kiss of peace to the people: 'Peace be with you.' It is Christ who gives the kiss to His Spouse, this being the symbol of the communion of the faithful among themselves—the peace—the union that leads back to Christ. According to Maximus the Confessor,

> the divine kiss is the sign of the union of all souls in God.... Through this union, those who are worthy of it enjoy intimacy with the Word and with God. For the mouth is the symbol of the word through which all men communicate with each other, being gifted with this faculty of the word and thereby participating in the sole Word, the cause of every word.[38]

And we shall conclude with a magnificent commentary by St Denis the Areopagite, which situates the rite of the kiss of peace within the ultimate perspective of the whole Divine Liturgy.

> We reverently exchange the most holy kiss of peace, for if we remain divided within ourselves, it is impossible to recollect ourselves in order to attain to the One, or participate in the peaceful unity of the One. If, on the contrary, thanks to the lights we receive from contemplation and knowledge of the One, we come to recollect ourselves and unite ourselves in a truly divine way,

38. *Mystagogy*, 1, 21; 17.

we will never more succumb to the diversity of those desires that foment material and passionate dissensions among fellow men. It seems to me therefore, that it is this unified and indivisible life that prescribes the sacred ceremony of the kiss of peace, basing anyone who assimilates himself to God in the very One who is the source of this assimilation.[39]

39. *The Ecclesiastical Hierarchy*, 3, 8.

Sculpted crosses, Ravenna, National Museum, fifth century.
Symbolic crucifixions: the Lamb, the Blessing Hand
between Sun and Moon.

Circular altar (Besançon Cathedral, eleventh century). The inscription that runs around the circumference: *Hoc signum praestat populis coelesta regna*: 'This is the sign that opens to the people the heavenly kingdom'; this sign is undoubtedly the monogram of Christ ☧ engraved at the center, but also perhaps the entire altar which 'is' Christ. On the circumference are arranged eight alveoli; now, eight is the number of Christ's resurrection.

Circular altar (Archeological Museum of Vienna, Austria).

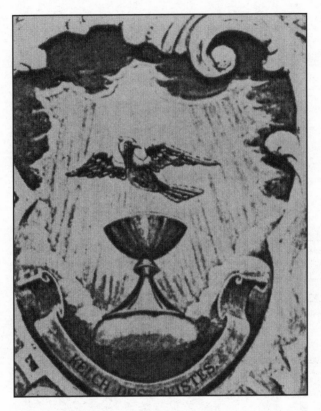

Epiclesis of the Holy Spirit, asking Him to consecrate by His Power
the Holy Blood in the chalice (ceiling painting from the church of
Grossmehring).

The so-called paten of Pulcheria, at the monastery of
Xeropotamou (from Kondakov, Athos)

Communion of the Apostles. Mosaic from Saint Sophia, Kiev.
(from Kondakov, *Rousskiia Drevnosti*)

Communion of the Apostles. Mosaic from Saint Sophia, Kiev
(from Kondakov, *Rousskiia Drevnosti*)

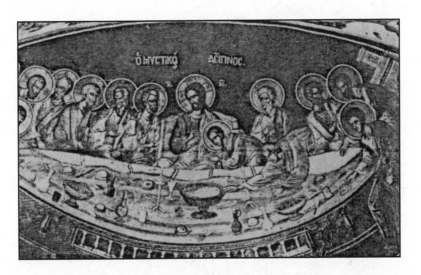

The Last Supper. Fresco from the Lavra refectory (Mount Athos), dated 1512. Judas, without halo, third to the left of Christ, reaches for a dish

Table altar (Mosaic from the Baptistery of St. Urso, Ravenna, fifth century)

Table altar (Mosaic from San Vitale, Ravenna) These monuments are the oldest reproductions of the altar in the West

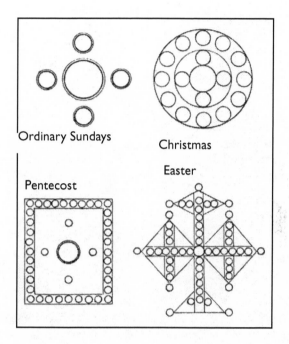

The arrangement of the bread oblations in the Mozarabic liturgy (Spain). On ordinary days only a single bread is used, on Sundays five, arranged in the form of a cross; on Christmas Day and certain other feasts, seventeen, five of which are placed in the form of a cross and the other twelve in a circle around them; on Easter and Pentecost forty-five breads are arranged in the pattern of a compound cross

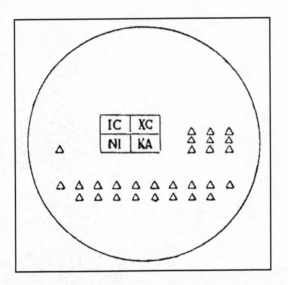

Arrangement of the eucharistic bread oblations on the diskos (paten) in the Greco-Byzantine Divine Liturgy: the morsels taken from the first three breads form a first row, the center of which is occupied the 'lamb' graven with the signs IC XC NI KA, while those intended for the living form a second row, and those devoted to the dead a third

Eucharistic celebration in the Coptic rite
Photo, 'Les coptes d'Egypte', Gérard Viaud (A. Maisonneuve)

Profession of faith before the communion of a Coptic priest
Photo, 'Les coptes d'Egypte', Gérard Viaud (A. Maisonneuve)

The *Sursum corda* in the Greek liturgy (*Anô tas kardias!*) before
the great Preface, the beginning of the eucharistic anaphora
Photo, 'Les liturgies catholiques orientales', Nicolas Liesel
(Letouzé et Ané

Elevation of the chalice after the Lord's Prayer during the Syrian Mass
'What is holy to the Holy! (Sancta scantis),
'One is the Father most holy, He who is with us, He who in His
goodness has created the world. Amen.
'One is the Son most holy, He who is with us, He has saved us
by the infinite worth of His sufferings. Amen.
'One is the Holy and Life-Giving Spirit, He who is with us, Creator and
Preserver of all things which are and were.
'May the name of the Lord be blessed, now and forever. Amen.'
Photo, 'Les liturgies catholiques orientales',
Nicolas Liesel (Letouzé et Ané)

Concelebration in the Melkite Greek Liturgy at St. Peter's,
Rome: the reading of the Epistle
Photo, 'Les liturgies catholiques orientales', Nicolas Liesel
(Letouzé et Ané)

4

The Altar
of the Lord

A MIMODRAMA is not an abstract creation detached from the conditions of time and place. The words and actions accomplished by its actors are linked to space and it cannot take place without a 'locus', which in a certain way is as necessary as the characters performing it. The 'locus' of the mimodrama of the Mass is the altar, which is the most sacred object in the temple, the reason for its existence and its very essence. One can, in cases of necessity, celebrate the divine liturgy outside of a church, but it is impossible to do so without a stone altar or, in the Byzantine rite, a substitute for the altar. This substitute, called the *antimension*, is a sacrosanct piece of cloth, upon which, moreover, the gifts are placed even when celebrating on an altar. According to Cabasilas, 'the altar is the beginning from which every sacred rite proceeds. The true temple is the altar . . . the rest of the building is only a complement, an imitation of the altar.'[1] We will get an idea of the eminent holiness of the altar by remembering the care taken in the ritual of its consecration.[2]

The altar's august holiness is not always apparent to the faithful ever since the Latin Church made it a long rectangular table, too often encumbered, moreover, with undesirable superstructures, while the altar is found improperly fastened to the wall of the apse.

1. Nicholas Cabasilas, *Life in Christ*, Fifth Book.
2. See, in particular, the number of *Maison-dieu* on *l'Autel* and, for the East, *Consécration et inauguration d'une église selon le rituel de l'Église russe* (rituel byzantine), Chevetogne, 1957.

The altar, in fact, is not simply a 'table', the table of the eucharistic banquet; it is also, and firstly, a 'stone', the stone of sacrifice.[3] In a strict sense the altar—what is called the 'fixed altar'—is a single natural stone resting on a base, also of stone, or at least four uprights of stone. In the case of a wooden altar, it is only the stone embedded in its center that merits the name of altar; this stone is moreover, properly speaking, a 'moveable altar'. The altar's true form is that of all primitive Christian altars, that is, a cubic altar, of small dimensions (edges of about 1 meter), composed of either a single solid stone, or as we have just said, a slab of stone on four columns of the same material (see ill.). This is still the case in the East, in those places, at least, where they have not tried to imitate the Latin Church, as too often happens, alas! Standing alone in the apse, thoroughly free of all inappropriate railings, adorned simply with the large illuminated cross and, possibly, some offerings of flowers, this altar has a truly hieratic appearance and a sacred character in conformity with the celebration that takes place there. For the Christian altar owes its sublimity to its celestial archetype, the Altar of the Heavenly Jerusalem, upon which the Lamb 'immolated from the beginning of the world' is outstretched. It is moreover the successor and synthesis of the Hebraic altars, as the Mass is the synthesis and sublimation of the sacrifices of the Old Law. What a striking correspondence there is, for example, between the altar raised by Moses at the foot of Sinai, where the blood of the victim was offered, half to God, the rest serving to sprinkle the people, in order to seal the First Covenant (Exod. 24:4–8), and the altar of the Mass, upon which the blood of

---

3. As early as the Apostolic Age, the two terms were employed concomitantly. St Paul speaks, in the same context of Cor. 10:14–21 of the 'table of the Lord' (*trapeza tou Kyriou*) and of participation at the 'altar' (*thysiastirion*); this last word is applied to the Cross in Heb. 13:10. The primitive use of ordinary tables for the Eucharist is explained by the historical circumstances, celebrations occurring at the beginning in private houses. But this primitive usage was abolished in the fifth century in both East and West. It is very instructive to recall that in England, a decree of 1550, renewed by Queen Elizabeth, ordered the replacement of the old altars of the churches with simple tables so as to be more in keeping with the representation of a simple commemorative meal (see J. Coblet, *Hist. du sacrement de l'Eucharistie*, Paris, 1886, vol. II, pp 66–67; J. Braun, *Der Christliche Altar*, Munich 1924, vol. I, p71; R. Zinhobler, *Linzer Theolog. Quartalschrift*, Heft 3, 1970, p147).

the New Covenant is poured out, offered to the Lord, then distributed to the people, sealing the reconciliation of man with God! In the temple at Jerusalem there were three altars. Between the court and the sanctuary stood the altar proper, that of the holocausts, where the daily sacrifice of the lamb was made. In the Sanctuary was the altar of incense, together with the seven-branched candlestick and the table of shewbreads, that is to say the offering. Finally, in the Holy of Holies, there was no altar properly speaking but a particularly sacred stone, the *shethiyah* stone, upon which the Ark of the Covenant rested before its disappearance. In the Christian temple, which replaces the temple of Jerusalem, the main altar is the synthesis of these different altars. It is the altar of holocausts, where the Lamb of God is sacrificed, as well as the table of shewbreads, that is to say the eucharistic bread. It is the altar of fragrances where incense is burned (we shall return to this). And finally, it is not exaggerated to say that it plays the role of the *shethiyah* stone supporting the Ark where the *Shekinah*, the 'Glory' or the 'Divine Presence', was manifested, for it is here that God makes Himself substantially present, and the more so in that the *Shekinah* has certain correspondences with the earthly manifestation of the Logos.[4]

The great preface of the Roman Pontifical for the consecration of an altar ritually links the Christian altar not only to that of Moses, but to those of Jacob and Abraham. Or more correctly, to all the altars of

)

---

4. The word *shekinah* is derived from the verb *shakan*, 'to dwell in a tent', the tent that served as temple to the Hebrews during their wandering in the desert and continued to designate the place of the Presence at Jerusalem. The Greek word *skene*, which served to translate *shekinah* in the Septuagint (for example Lev. 23:34, 2 Macc. 10:6), is perhaps not without etymological connection to the Hebrew word, replicating the three consonants of the root word. In any case, this 'assonance' is full of meaning from the point of view of what can be called symbolic etymology. What is altogether remarkable, as regards the correspondences of the Son of God incarnate and the *Shekinah*, is that the Gospel of St John (1:4) uses precisely the Greek word *skenoun*, the exact translation of *shakan*, to say that the Word made Flesh 'dwelt among us'; *ho logos eskenosen en himin*; *eskenosen*, that is to say, literally, 'pitched his tent'. See, concerning this subject, L. Bouyer, *La Shekinah: Dieu avec nous*, 'Bible et Vie chretienne', 20, 1957, p7 ff.

humanity, from that of Abel right up to Melchizedek.[5] There is reason to dwell somewhat upon the altar of Jacob, because we see in it an absolutely essential aspect of the altar in general and its symbolism.

The point from which to start is Jacob's anointing of the *Bethel Stone* (*Gen.* 28:11–19). One night, on his way to Mesopotamia, Jacob lay down to sleep, directly on the ground using a stone for a pillow. While asleep he dreamed he saw a ladder set up on earth, reaching to heaven, upon which angels ascended and descended and above which stood the Eternal. When he awoke, he cried out, 'How dreadful is this place! It is none other than the house of God (*Beth-El*) and the gate of heaven.' And to commemorate his vision, he poured oil over the stone thereby making it an altar. In the ritual of consecration, the pontiff repeats the action of the Patriarch by pouring holy oils over the sacred stone while an anthem recalling Jacob's action is sung. Thus the stone of the altar is ritually assimilated to the stone of Jacob.

If this stone is surrounded with such veneration, this is because it conceals a great mystery, which resides in the fact that it is situated at the 'center of the world'.[6] The notion of the 'center of the world' is basic to numerous rites in all religions. This 'center' is not a geographic center at least in the sense of the modern science of geography, but a symbolic center (which does not mean imaginary, quite the contrary) based on geometric symbolism. If the universe is represented as a sphere or a circle, the center will be the most important point, for it is what engenders the whole figure. In the spiritual sense, then, one symbolically situates at the 'center of the world' and upon the 'axis of the world', every sacred place or object that allows one to make contact with the Spiritual Center, that is to say God Himself, who is the center, the beginning and end of the whole sphere of creation.

5. One cannot over-exaggerate the importance of Melchizedek from every point of view concerning the Judeo-Christian tradition, for it is through him that the Jewish people, before Moses, received the deposit of original orthodoxy.

6. According to tradition, the stone of Jacob was taken to Mount Zion where it became the rock of Ornan over which David erected the altar of holocausts. This is *Al-Sakhra*, 'the Rock' that can be seen today in the Mosque of Omar. See Ch. Ledit, *La Mosquée sur le Roc*, Tetraktys, 1966.

The altar of Jacob is situated at the 'center of the world', as the sacred text gives us to understand when it speaks of the 'angelic ladder'. This ladder represents the 'world axis', the bottom of which rests on the earth while its top constitutes the 'gate of heaven', and is the natural path of the angels as 'messengers' of Heaven on earth and executors of the Will of Heaven. The altar embodies the point of intersection of the axis with the surface of the earth.

Thus, through the rite of consecration, the Christian altar, like that of Jacob, becomes the 'center of the world' and is situated on the heaven-earth axis, which makes it a fitting place for a theophany, a divine manifestation, the place where heaven and earth meet. This is the place that the Son of God chose in order to offer Himself for us, as it is written in the Psalms: 'For God is my king of old, working salvation in the midst of the earth' (Psalm 73). Through this sacrifice He re-establishes the axial communication with God, re-opens the 'gate of heaven', and truly makes the temple a *bethel*, a 'house of God'.

We said above there was a sacrosanct stone in the temple at Jerusalem termed *shethiyah* upon which the Ark rested. This stone, too, represented the 'center of the World'. The term *shethiyah* means 'foundational' and, according to the Hebraic tradition, it is upon this stone that God builds the world. It is the center of the great cosmic circle, which is why the Holy of Holies and, by extension, the whole city of Jerusalem was situated at the 'center of the world'. Now, there can be no doubt that the altar stone, and the altar as a whole, has definite connections with the *shethiyah* stone, as we shall soon see. Let us say immediately that the cosmic diagram of the cardinal directions is reproduced on the altar stone: in fact there are five crosses engraved upon it, one at each corner and one at the center. 'The four crosses,' says Durandus of Mende, 'signify that Christ redeemed the four quarters of the world. . . . The cross in the middle of the altar signifies that the Saviour accomplished our redemption at the center of the world, that is to say at Jerusalem.'[7] But there is more; the altar stone and the altar are assimilated to Christ Himself. All the Fathers agree on this point. St Ignatius of Antioch

7. *Rationale*, I, 7.

writes, 'All of you hasten to unite in the same temple of God, at the foot of the same altar, that is to say in Jesus Christ.'[8] According to St Cyril of Jerusalem, the altar is Christ because, 'Christ is the chosen stone, the corner stone, the precious stone.'[9] Likewise, Simeon of Thessalonica: 'The altar symbolizes Jesus as the 'Rock of Life' (*pet-ran zois*) and the 'corner stone' (*lithon gonias*).'[10]

This identification of the altar with Christ seems to be expressly based on a passage from Scripture that says, speaking of Christ, 'We have an altar' (Heb. 13:10). This passage should in turn be approached from the famous verses of the *First Epistle to the Corinthians* (10:1–4):

All our fathers were under the cloud, and all passed through the sea; and were all baptized unto Moses ... and did all eat the same spiritual meat; and did all drink the same spiritual drink: for they drank of the spiritual rock that followed them: and that rock was Christ [*hi petra de in ho Christos*].

This affirmation of St Paul is in the most authentic Hebraic tradition. For ages the Lord was assimilated to the stone and the rock, and from it the Israelites were said to be drawn: 'Of the rock that begat thee thou art unmindful, and hast forgotten God that formed thee' (Deut. 32:18). 'Look unto the rock whence you are hewn, and to the hole of the pit whence you are digged' (Isa. 51:1). This symbolism of the stone is also related to the Messiah. Isaiah's text, 'Behold, I lay in Zion for a foundation a stone, a tried stone, a precious corner stone, a sure foundation: he that believeth shall not make haste' (Isa. 28:16) is applied to the Messiah by St Peter (1 Pet. 2:5 –6) and St Paul (Rom. 9:33).[11]

---

8. *Ad Magnes*, 6.

9. PG 68, 592–593 and 647.

10. *De sacro templo*, 107 (PG 155, 313). Cf. Hesychius of Jerusalem (PG 93, 796–797 and 828); St Ephrem, *Hom. on the Crucifixion* (Lamy I, 660); Simeon the New Theologian, *De sacra liturgia*, 98 (P.G. 155, 293); Moses Bar-Kepha, *Expl. of the Myst.of the Oblation* (Connoly, 675); Denis Bar-Salibi, *Explan. of the Liturgy*, C.S.S.O 93, pp87 and 93.

11. We are summarizing here the considerations we developed on the relations between the *foundation stone* and the *cornerstone* in our *Symbolism of the Christian*

Thus Christ is simultaneously the 'foundation stone' (*shethiyah*) and the 'cornerstone' (*rosh ha-pinnah*, in Hebrew). The foundation stone is cubic and in the architectural domain, symbolizes the earth; on the spiritual plane it is the Word in the world. The cornerstone, or keystone of the vault, situated at the summit of the building, has a 'heavenly' aspect and represents Christ glorified, seated at the right hand of the Father and 'completing the construction' of the Church. In the temple, the cornerstone in the vault, or key of the vault, 'the summit of the angle', corresponds to the *shethiyah* stone (altar) below. The two stones are situated on the same vertical line, which is the 'axial pillar'. This pillar is 'virtual', in the sense that it is not embodied (except in the case of pendentive vault keys, which constitute the beginnings of embodiment), which does not prevent it from playing a primordial role, since it is around it that the whole edifice is laid out. It represents the world axis.

Finally, all this symbolism is repeated and precisely stated in the canopy or baldachin. The latter, made up of a dome supported on four columns, is a piece of furniture that should in principle cover the main altar. (Many churches are still faithful to this requirement of the baldachin.) The basic design of the baldachin is a cube (the four columns) surmounted by a hemisphere, that is to say the very pattern of the sanctuary, of the whole temple and the universe (heaven above the earth). How better to suggest that the altar is at the center of the world?

The axial pillar joining the two Christic stones is the 'way of salvation'; the key of the vault is the 'gate of heaven' (*janua coeli*) like the summit of Jacob's Ladder. Cosmologically, this axis is the World Axis, and theologically, the Way, that is to say, Christ Himself, who said: 'I am the Way.'

The axial character of the position of the altar is further underlined by another symbolism. The steps, which are required for the

Temple, pp 87–104. The Christic symbolism of the stone is underlined by the fact that in Hebrew the word designating stone *aben* (pronounced 'eben') blends with *aben*, the emphatic form of *ben*, signifying 'son'. Let us note again that the number of *aben* and that of *dabar*, 'the Word', obtained through reduction is the same: 8. And the triple repetition of this number, 888, is that of the name of Jesus in Greek: IHCYOC.

erecting of an altar, recall that the latter stands on the 'Holy Mountain', which is an image of the world and of paradise.[12] This is already indicated by the liturgy of the Mass when right at the beginning it has the priest recite the Psalm *Judica me* (Psalm 42) that the Israelites chanted while climbing Mount Zion to go to the Temple: 'O send out thy light and thy truth; let them lead me; let them bring me unto thy *holy hill*, and to thy tabernacles. Then will I go *unto the altar of God*.' The Christian altar is also Mount Zion where the Upper Room was situated. Even more is it the hill of Golgotha, where Christ was offered as victim on the altar of the Cross, which is concretely recalled by the large crucifix standing on the Christian altar for the celebration of Divine Liturgy. And if this sacrifice took place on Golgotha, this certainly has a meaning, also linked to the spiritual meaning of the mountain. This is suggested by the fact that it was to a mountain that Christ often retired to pray. And on a mountain that he accomplished the essential acts of his mission: the Sermon on the Mount, the Transfiguration on Mount Thabor and both the Agony and the Ascension on the Mount of Olives.

The mountain belongs in the category of those great universal symbols, constituting the natural language of every sacred action and every liturgy. The mountain is in fact a striking image. It is where the earth comes closest to heaven. Vertical, its summit reaching towards heaven, it invites ascension to God; surrounded by clouds, the seat of terrible storms, it appears as a privileged manifestation of divine power; it is both the place of theophany and the symbol of our spiritual ascension. Reduced to its basic design, the pyramid, it is a volume disposed about an axis. A self-sufficient volume, offering thus a resumé of the world: rooted in the earth, resting on the surface, touching heaven with which it is mysteriously joined by the lightning, it links together, through its axis, the three 'stories' of the world: hell, earth, and heaven. This axis is identified

12. Let us immediately respond to the objection of those who see nothing in the steps but a way of raising the altar and thereby making it more visible to the congregation, by saying that the symbolism does not suppress the utilitarian role and, inversely, that the latter does not suppress the symbolism, at least true symbolism, because the latter belongs to the very nature of things; which is evident in the case before us.

with the World Axis. Herein lies the explanation of the various traditions relating to the cosmic mountain which is nearly always identified with Paradise. In Iran, Mount Alborj marks the center of the world; there the fountain of life forms a lake in the center of which stands the Tree of Life—another axial symbol. From the lake the waters descend in four rivers to the four regions of space. In India, Mount Meru is the highest point on earth, the point where one reaches heaven. It is the center of everything and the North Pole, that is to say the fixed pole of the world. One also finds a lake on top of Meru in which the water of life is collected, and a garden of delights with the Tree of Beatitude, the apple tree. Here, there and everywhere, the holy mountain is where the ark of salvation came to rest after the flood (that of Noah, for example, came to rest on the summit of Ararat), and it is from this summit that the new humanity set out. Marking the axis of the world, where heaven and earth unite, the mountain plays a symbolic role in religious rites analogous to that of the stone and the tree. Certainly it is often at the top of a mountain, representing the cosmic mountain, that altars were raised and temples built. It is known, furthermore, that the Hindu temple is modeled on Mount Meru, which it reproduces in its basic architectural design. The steps permit one to ascend right to the summit and the faithful who avail themselves of them make a ritual ascent to heaven, the summit being identified with the latter, since it is at the top of the cosmic mountain that the original paradise was situated. Durandus of Mende expresses the same idea regarding the Christian altar. The steps of the altar, he says, recall the fifteen steps leading to the Temple of Solomon which one climbs while singing the fifteen psalms called 'the psalms of the steps'. They both, he continues, symbolize the fifteen virtues that lead to heaven, which is why the steps are also those of Jacob's Ladder, which also lead to heaven.[13]

---

13. Durandus of Mende, *Rationale* I, 2. It is probably because of the number of steps of Solomon's Temple that those of the altar are required to be uneven. In general there are *three* steps corresponding to the constitutive ternary of man: body, soul, and spirit. This does not detract from the ascensional symbolism, because it is to these three elements of the human microcosm that the three higher levels of the macrocosm correspond: earth, air, and empyrean. These in turn correspond to the

In light of the above, the Sacrifice of Calvary takes on a striking relief. Jesus chose that His death, through which the new creation was effected, take place on a mountain, the synthetic image, center and summit of the world, on that axis that links earth to heaven and where the original Paradise re-appears. The full symbolism of the mountain of salvation has often been treated in early and Byzantine Christian art. One sees Christ standing or seated at the summit of the mountain whence rise the paradisal rivers; sometimes He is seated in the Tree of Life, fused with the Cross, next to which the Fountain of Life, divided into four branches, gushes forth. Christ, the new Adam, restores paradise. He is the Tree of Life and the Source from which the living waters of eternal Life gush forth to the four regions of the universe. This image is a wonderful plastic expression of the eucharistic mystery, which renews the sacrifice of Golgotha, restores the world to its primordial purity and re-establishes communication between heaven and earth. So then, when, after the first prayers of the Mass, the priest ascends to the altar, he climbs the Mountain of Salvation and goes to renew, at the center and summit of the world, the sacrifice intended to save it.

The symbolism of the altar is also expressed on another plane, that of light. Lighted candles on the altar are obligatory for the celebration of the Divine Liturgy because Christ is 'the Light of the World'. In the Syrian liturgy, the lighting of the candles is part of the office itself and during this rite two beautiful prayers are chanted:

> Through Thy light we see light, O Jesus, full of light. Thou art the true Light lighting all creatures, enlighten us with Thy beautiful Light, O icon of the heavenly Father.

> O Pure and Holy One, who livest in the spheres of light, remove far from us evil passions and impure thoughts. Grant that we may perform the works of righteousness with purity of heart.

---

three planes of existence: material, subtle, and spiritual, and under a different relationship, to the three degrees of initiation (in Christianity: baptism, confirmation, and eucharist).

But this general meaning of candles in themselves is coupled with a particular meaning arising from their number. There should be six candles on the altar, three on each side of the cross. Now, it is nearly certain that these *six* candles should in fact be *seven*, as is proved particularly by the rule for an episcopal Mass, which requires *seven* candles, and the practice of the Byzantines who use a proper chandelier of seven branches. At any rate, the central cross plays the role of the seventh candle, as we are going to see. This arrangement of lights is the Christian version of the Hebrew seven branched candlestick, called the *menorah*, made up of a straight central branch and six curved branches arranged in three concentric semi-circles. The seven branches were linked together by means of inner ducts that were filled with a consecrated olive oil that fed the lamps. Like the Ark, the *menorah* was made according to a heavenly model seen by Moses on the mountain (Num. 8:4; cf. Exod. 25:34, 37:20–23; Lev. 24:2–4, Num. 8:3–4). If the *menorah* has passed to the Christian cult, this is because it also belongs to the New Testament. In the *Apocalypse*, in fact, Christ appears surrounded by *seven* candlesticks (Apoc. 2:1) and this apparition resembles not a little that seen by the prophet Zechariah (Zech. 3:9). The number of the lamps, *seven*, has a cosmological and a theological meaning. Seven, considered as 3 + 4, is the sign of the relations of the Divine with Creation, 3 and 4 being the divine and created world respectively. Whence the *seven days* of Creation, the expression in *time* of the relations of the uncreated and created, of which the *seven planets* are the *spatial* expression. Philo and Clement of Alexandria affirm that the seven branches of the menorah represent the planets, the one in the middle being the sun, which gives its light to all. Clement, for his part, identified it with Christ, 'the Sun of Righteousness',[14] for the cosmic symbolism conceals a theological symbolism. The latter is based on the mystical doctrine of the *Sephiroth* that one finds in St John.[15]

The *Sephiroth*, which are the aspects of the Divinity, or even its Energies, are ten in number, divided into two groups: the three

14. Philo, *Vit. Mos.* 2, 102 ff.; Clem. of Alex. *Strom.* v 6, 34, 8 ff.
15. See A. Frank-Duquesne in *Cahiers du symbolisme chrétien* 3, 1938.

higher *sephiroth* relate to the Divine Nature while the seven lower are the Attributes of God, or again the Energies or Powers which preside at the Creation. The lower *sephiroth* are the irradiations of God, the influences that He spreads over the universe, the lights whereby the Unfathomable is revealed, the instruments wherewith the Divine Architect constructs the Creation and maintains its harmony.

The *sephiroth* are commonly called 'Voices', 'Thunders', 'Lamps' and 'Eyes', and this enables us to understand the passage from the Apocalypse (5:6) where it is said that the Lamb has seven eyes which are the seven spirits of God. These 'eyes' are the same as the 'seven bright lamps' burning before the throne (4:5). In parallel fashion, in the prophecy of Zechariah (3:9), seven eyes are engraved on the mysterious stone, mentioned above, designating the Messiah. In all these cases, it is a question of the seven lower *sephiroth* or creative powers of God and, in particular, of the Divine Word.

It is easy, then, to understand the deep meaning of the lights on the altar.

The seven lights (more often reduced to six, the seventh being united with the central crucifix) recall the seven spiritual lights before the heavenly throne of Christ. They represent the total world and, more exactly, the world transfigured by the divine presence of Christ, whose seven powers are active within it. This world restored to its purity only exists today in the precinct of the sanctuary and thanks to the divine effect of the Mass. This spiritualized world, indicated by the lamps, is finally the Church and the Mystical Body: the Church with its seven sacraments, issued from the altar, the Stone with seven eyes! illuminating the faithful and uniting them to form the Mystical Body which is already 'the new heavens and the new earth'.

The divine liturgy of the Mass fully realizes the meaning of the Hebraic liturgy, in particular that of the Feast of Tabernacles and the Sabbath. The Feast of Tabernacles (*Sukkot*) extended over seven days consecrated to the seven Patriarchs, who 'incarnate' the seven *sephiroth* watching over the harmony of the world. Likewise, the liturgy of the Sabbath or seventh day celebrated universal equilibrium through the blessings descending from the seven *sephiroth* or spirits of God.

In Roman churches, the relation between the lights of the altar and the heavenly candlestick of the Apocalypse was sometimes underlined by the pictures decorating the vault of the apse above the altar. This vault, the image of the heavenly dome, regularly bore the icon of the Pantocrator seated on the Royal Throne. Now, in certain cases, for example in the crypt of Saint Etienne of Auxerre, the heavenly candlestick of seven branches was painted before the throne of Christ. Thus was suggested, by means of a really sacred art, the object of the liturgy, which, through the altar, re-establishes communication between heaven and earth and causes the grace and peace sprung from the Sevenfold Light to descend upon the world in order to renew it.

It is again light that determines another aspect of the altar: we have in mind its orientation. We broach here a problem that is in itself very important, but in our days has become even more so as a result of the polemic that has arisen around this subject.

The altar should be oriented regularly to the East, therefore towards the apse in normal churches, that is to say churches that are likewise oriented to the East. Let us also hasten to say that the orientation of the temple is a consequence of the orientation of the altar and that the latter, in its turn, is a consequence of the orientation of prayer.[16] We should begin, in fact, from there. The primordial fact, governing everything else, is this: the priest, and the faithful, pray and sacrifice facing the East. This rule is attested from earliest Christian antiquity, for example in the *Apostolic Constitutions* (2, 7). We also read that Hipparchus, a member of the first Judeo-Christian communities, had a room in his house arranged for prayer. On its eastern wall a cross was painted, and there, seven times a day, he prayed *with face turned to the East*.[17] The antiquity of this rule of prayer and the progressive generalizing of the orientation of

16. See J. Hani, op. cit., pp34–40.
17. *The Acts of Hipparchus and Philotheus* cited in J. Daniélou, *The Theology of Jewish Christianity*, 1964, pp268–269.

churches, which soon took place, is today a well-established fact, to which there is no need to return.[18]

Orientation for prayer and sacrifice is not peculiar to Christianity; it is universal and, in all religions, minutely regulated. The reason for this is that every human act, but more especially every sacred act, should be executed in harmony with the cosmic ambience. The latter, while exerting certain subtle influences over man and his actions, which it is not at all good to neglect, is at the same time full of symbols that 'speak' to man of the divine and help him to concentrate all his spiritual powers upon the deed to be executed.

This is very especially so with light and the sun, which have always and everywhere been the privileged symbols of Divinity. God is light and quite naturally natural light leads us to this superessential Light. The light of the sun is the cause of vision and sensible knowledge and at the same time physical life, as God is the cause of knowledge and life for the spirit. 'For with thee,' says the Psalmist, 'is the fountain of life; in thy light we shall see light (Psalm 35). But particular attention should be given to the movement of the sun. Its daily course punctuates life on earth, while its different 'stations' in the signs of the Zodiac determine the year and the seasons, and, at a much higher level, the great cycles of the evolution of humanity. In orienting prayer and sacrifice, it is essentially the daily cycle that is taken into consideration and especially the rising sun, the sign of the rebirth of life. Again the Psalmist says:

> The heavens declare the glory of God; and the firmament showeth his handiwork. . . . In them hath he set a tabernacle for the sun, which is as a bridegroom coming out of his chamber, and rejoiceth as a strong man to run a race. His going forth is from the end of the heaven, and his circuit unto the ends of it: and there is nothing hid from the heat thereof (Psalm 18).

18. On this subject, see the definitive studies of Cyril Vogel, 'Sol aequinoctalis', *Rev. d. Sc. Relig.*, 1962, 175–211; 'Versus ad Orientem', *La Maison-Dieu*, 70, 1962, 67–99; 'L'orientation vers l'Est'. *L'Orient syrien*, 9, 1964, 3–35. And earlier: E. Peterson, 'La croce e la preghiera verso l'Oriente'. *Ephemer. liturg.* 59, 1945.

Such is the profound reason for liturgical orientation: 'The east,' says Clement of Alexandria,

> is the image of the birth of the day. It is from this quarter that the light increases, rising in the same way that the sun rises from the shadows where ignorance stagnates and whence the day of the knowledge of truth is liberated. Accordingly it is normal that prayers be directed towards the birth of the dawn.[19]

In the Old Testament the symbol of the rising sun received an extraordinary confirmation in one of Ezekiel's visions. The prophet, led by God to the eastern gate of the temple, saw 'the Glory of the God of Israel [which] came from the way of the east.... And the glory of the Lord came into the house by the way of the gate whose prospect is toward the east' (Ezek. 43:2, 4). Genesis, for its part, teaches us that the primordial Paradise was situated to the east (Gen. 2:8). And Christ, who said, 'I am the light of the world' (John 8:12), was announced by the prophets as the 'rising sun' and 'the sun of righteousness' (Mal. 3:20); in Zechariah, God said, in speaking of the Messiah: 'I will bring my servant the Orient' (Zech. 3:8), a motif remembered later by the other Zechariah, who, when taking the infant Messiah in his arms, proclaimed 'the dayspring from on high hath visited us, to give light to them that sit in darkness and in the shadow of death, to guide our feet into the way of peace' (Luke 1:78–80). Finally, in the New Testament, the east has assumed a clearly eschatological character. Has not Christ announced His return at the end of time in these terms? 'For as the lightning cometh out of the east, and shineth even unto the west; so shall also the coming of the Son of man be' (Matt. 24, 27). He also said that at the moment of His Parousia one will see 'the sign of the Son of Man' (*Ibid.* 30) appearing in heaven, that is to say the Cross that St Ephrem celebrates in one of his hymns 'as the scepter of Christ the great King... surpassing the sun in brightness and preceding the coming of the Master of all things.' This is why the first Christian communities, as we remarked above regarding Hipparchus, placed a cross on the eastern wall of their places of prayer; in this way during the course

19. *Strom*, 7, 7. Cf. Origen, *De orat.* P. G. 11, 555.

of their offices their gaze tended towards this anticipation of the Parousia. The practice continued during the first centuries and became the source of those magnificent apses decorated with mosaics showing an immense golden cross on a background of a starstudded sky, as for example at San Vitale in Ravenna. The decoration of the apse vault with the Pantocrator, the image of Christ in glory from the Apocalypse mentioned above is the same eschatological symbolism, under a different form, offered to later ages.

This rule of temple orientation should clarify and resolve the irritating problem of the Mass celebrated 'facing the people'. In fact, since the Latin Church undertook its famous liturgical reform, we have seen another altar everywhere springing up in front of the old main altar. More often than not it is a sort of wooden table, oriented in the opposite direction from the old altar, that is to say turned towards the congregation, so as to enable the priest to celebrate facing the faithful. The promoters of this way of doing things, who apparently see in it a way of strengthening the bond between celebrant and faithful, have attempted to justify their reform by claiming that this was the original way of celebrating the Mass. But their argument is altogether specious. It is true, certainly, that in the majority of Roman basilicas, and in particular at St Peters, one celebrated, and even today continues to celebrate the Mass at an altar situated at the crossing of the transept and facing the congregation. The true reason for this state of affairs is that these basilicas, constructed according to the custom of the ancient Romans, have their entrances to the east and their apses to the west. As a result, the celebrant *turned towards the east* and, by that very fact, found that he was facing the faithful. But, in correctly oriented churches, the celebrant, for the same reason of orientation, turned his back to the congregation. There was never at the beginning any theory whatsoever of a Mass 'facing the people'; orientation was the sole concern. And so the argument advanced by the promoters of the current liturgical reform is simply an archeological oversight, which backfires upon those who, generally, profess to mock the rule of orientation. It is to avoid the inconvenience—for as we shall see, there is one—presented by the Roman basilicas, that one was everywhere advised to construct, in imitation of the countries of the East, churches with their apse to the east. In this way, altar, celebrant and congregation are turned in the same authentically sacred direction, since it is founded on Scripture and, what is more, is canonical, which seems to be forgotten. In effect, the inconvenience, in the case of Rome, consisted in the fact that if the celebrant was regularly oriented, the faithful for their part, were not. Now, the matter is important, because, in the oldest Christian symbolism—as also in the majority of traditions—the west is the region of the dead and of shadows, from the fact that it is the place where the sun disappears. We know that in the ancient ritual of baptism, the candidate was solemnly invited to turn to the west to pronounce his renunciation of sin and the Devil, symbolically situated in that direction, then to turn towards the east, that is, towards the Christ-Sun, to inaugurate his new life.[20] Now, this very East-West line constitutes the principal axis of the Christian Temple. The baptistery is constructed to the west for it is the place of passage out of the shadows. It is the place of the bath, the symbol of the Red Sea, that one must pass through in order to quit the world of shadows and death and be in a position, then, to undertake a march to the light. The newly baptized, after the baptismal bath, enter the temple in procession, and march in the direction of the altar, which, like the apse, is situated to the east and represents the kingdom of eternal light. And it is also this direction that should dictate the position of the Christian assembly and the celebrant for the Divine Liturgy, which itself is a march towards the Christic light and an anticipation of the eschatological Kingdom.

This is why in correctly oriented churches, to say Mass 'facing the people' by turning one's back to the light, is an aberration, and graver than is believed, for it effects a veritable rupture of that just referred to movement from the shadows to the light. We are faced with an inversion of the symbol. Now, the inversion of symbols is a serious matter. Actually, those who say Mass in this way are probably none the wiser, but the small group of those who decided this reform knew what they were doing. Or, at least, were 'guided' by others who 'knew' and possessed the means to push them to it

---

20. St Cyril of Jerusalem, *Mystag. Catech.* 19, 1 (P.G. 33, 1074).

through certain 'suggestions', without, moreover, the 'subjects' being aware of it. All this, obviously, is barely understandable to the majority of our contemporaries, including the hierarchical Church right up to its highest representatives, who are no longer aware either of the real nature of the symbol, or, above all, of its potentialities. When a symbol, sacralized by means of a rite and a spiritual influence, is voluntarily inverted, it risks, almost certainly, vehicling an influence opposite in nature to the first. It is a case here of saying: 'Let those who have ears to hear, hear!'

In churches that are not oriented—which unfortunately is ever more often the case since the sixteenth century—to look for the correct orientation to celebrate is difficult or impossible. Most often the apse is not even to the east, but directed to the north or south or even along an intermediate line. The only solution is, as always, to act as if the apse were truly to the east, and celebrate in that direction. One can always, in such a case, consider that the apse and the altar are symbolically to the east, if, at least—but this is not always the case—the altar is surmounted, according to the rule, with the cross, announcing the Second Coming. Thus the Divine Liturgy will be celebrated 'facing God',[21] which, whatever the case, is more valuable than 'facing the people', for is not the goal of the Holy Sacrifice to lead the people before the Face of the Lord?

The orientation of the priest towards the east integrates him and the whole celebration into a cosmic pattern: space qualified by the lines joining the four cardinal points, the cross that 'crucifies the world'. This integration is necessary because man, being a bodily creature and part of the cosmos, needs to be in harmony with the latter, as much upon the material as upon the subtle plane. In the present case, priest and congregation are in harmony particularly with the movement of the sun, the master of both space and time.

21. This is the title of J.J. Fournée's excellent little book, *La Messe face à Dieu*, Coll. 'Una Voce' 5, Paris, 1976; this work, perfectly documented, offers, in some forty pages, an exposition of all the problems and their reasonable solution.

But the liturgy's integration into the cosmic order goes much further still. Even a quick analysis of a certain number of the key words and gestures punctuating the unfolding of the Divine Liturgy, will enable us to verify this.

If, for example, we take that of the Roman Mass, we see that its *sequences* are developed around repetitive *patterns*, of which there are also two, which dictate its structure as a whole and finally determine its meaning.

In the preparatory prayers at the foot of the altar there are three striking elements. The psalm, *Judica me*, evokes the 'holy mountain', to which the celebrant asks God to lead him; the *Confiteor* is addressed to the whole of the heavenly court, and finally, the prayers terminate with a supplication to God: 'May my cry reach even unto You!' The singing of the *Gloria* is summed up in the first verse 'Glory to God in the highest heavens and peace on earth to men.' The *Credo* is addressed to God, 'creator of heaven and earth', then it evokes the Son who 'descended from heaven and become man', 'died, descended into hell, rose and ascended to heaven' whence he 'shall come again'. At the offertory, the priest raises the bread and the chalice towards heaven; he prays the Holy Spirit to 'come' and 'bless' the Gifts. The rite of the censing first evokes heaven anew, with the altar of the incense, to the right of which the archangel Michael stands, after which the celebrant censes while saying: 'May this incense ascend to You and Thy mercy descend upon us.' The start of the great eucharistic prayer is marked by the invitation of the *Sursum corda*: 'Lift up your hearts!' and the response: 'We lift them up unto the Lord!' The preface constitutes a veritable unveiling of the heavenly court, where the angels chant the praise of God, to whose voices we on earth join ours. This is the chanting of the Sanctus and the evocation of the Divine Glory filling heaven and earth, with a further appearance of the heavenly court during the canon with the prayer *Communicantes*. At the consecration the priest repeats the words and actions of Christ 'while lifting his eyes to heaven'. In the sacrifice that is accomplished, the anamnesis recalls the death of the Lord, His descent into hell, His resurrection, and His ascension. Then the prayer *Supra quae respicere* inserts the sacrifice of the Mass into the line of previous sacrifices since Abel. The prayer *Supplices* asks God to send His angel to take the Holy Gifts and carry them to the heavenly altar. There follows the *Memento*, the propitiatory prayer for the deceased who still *sleep*, that they might be granted entry into the place of peace and of *light* (= heaven), and, in the *Nobis quoque peccatoribus*, a new and third appearance of the heavenly court to which the priest asks that we may one day be admitted. Finally the Lord's Prayer summons anew the coming of the Kingdom on *earth* as in *heaven*. To these different sequences of words all the gestures of the priest should properly be added. The most characteristic are the arms held out horizontally like a cross, when praying, and the gestures of elevation, the elevation of the eyes to heaven, and of the gifts, which we have already mentioned.[22]

It is evident from this analysis that the Mass unfolds according to a dual pattern which determines its internal structure: a horizontal pattern and a vertical pattern. The *horizontal* pattern is related to the earth: it encompasses the celebrant and the congregation, not only of such and such a temple and time, but all the priests and all the faithful who, at that moment throughout the world, are offering the sacrifice. Let us go further; this horizontal pattern is that of *time*, the measure of the world's manifestation, from Adam in the past right up until the Parousia. The Roman Mass, as we have just seen, evokes the time of Abel; the Syrian Mass commemorates 'our father Adam and our mother Eve.' This pattern, that of the Church Militant, constitutes in the final count a ritual integration of the whole

---

22. It is impossible to study all the officiant's movements here; such a study would nevertheless be very interesting because, like all ritual movements and postures, the movements of the priest are charged with meaning in relation to the rite. We shall only say a word about the gesture which, together with that of the extended arms, occurs most frequently during the mass: the hands held together. This gesture is the opposite to that of the extended arms. It has a dual symbolism. First of all the hands, which are the *operative* members, being brought together, are immobilized and, at the same time, the circuit of energies, which, we know, escapes from the open hands is closed; this favors concentration and adorative meditation. Furthermore, the two hands pressed together make but one; the two polarities, of the man of the right and the man of the left, are symbolically reduced to unity. Finally, if we consider the fingers of the hand, which are 5 in number and which give a total of 10, one sees that, with the hands together, one has $10 = 1 + 0 = 1$, another concrete expression of unity.

of cosmic duration. The *vertical* pattern concerns the other world in
its two modalities: heaven and the hells. At the top of the vertical
line is God, the Angels, and the Elect, or the Church Triumphant,
while at the bottom the 'place' of the dead who are not yet entirely
delivered and constitute the Church Suffering. The combination of
these two patterns translates immediately into the following figure:

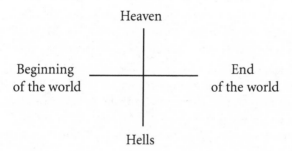

If now, one relates this figure, which integrates the two patterns
of which we have just spoken, to the figure relating to the orientation of the priest and the altar, the figure giving the four cardinal
directions *in the horizontal plane*;

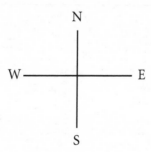

one is led to effect a second integration, which will be that of the two
figures: the vertical axis of heaven and hell of the first is,
cosmologically, the line joining the two poles of the universe
represented materially by the pole star and the southern cross; the

horizontal, or temporal axis, merges with the horizontal plane of the second figure, that of the cardinal points. In this figure, the two lines, east-west and north-south, that we always consider in the horizontal plane, correspond, relatively, to the two lines joining, respectively, the two equinoctial points and the two solstitial points. This is the horizontal cross, constituting the plane within which the sun moves in its daily and annual movements, and it is because of this that it is the plane of time. The vertical axis, or the polar axis, perpendicular to the heavenly equator, coincides exactly, in our definitive integration, with the intersection point of the lines joining the cardinal points. The two figures are perfectly joined and thereby give a structure of six dimensions, called a solid, or even volumetric, cross. The ensemble of these two integrated crosses with the same center, defines the structure of space (*per se*) and of a space qualified by the cardinal directions related as well to the movement of the temporal cycle and the sun around the Immobile Axis, the World Axis, the image of the 'Unmoved Mover'. The branches of this solid cross constitute the six directions of space, which with the center itself, form the septenary. Now, the directions of space correspond to the Divine Attributes, as polarization—in relation to a center—of undifferentiated space, which is like the Divine Unity. Clement of Alexandria tells us, in effect, that from God, the 'Heart of the Universe' indefinite extensions move outwards, above and below, to the right and left, and to the front and back.

Simultaneously and forever directing His gaze towards these six extensions, He completes the world; He is the beginning and the end; in Him the six phases of time are completed, and it is from Him that they receive their indefinite extension: this is the secret of the number *Seven*.

Elsewhere [23] we have shown that this cross determines the structure of the Christian temple. This latter structure, however, is in the first place a *gestural structure*, that of the celebration of the Holy Mass, such that the temple where it takes place is only the crystallization of the *gestural* dynamic of liturgical celebration, which

23. J. Hani, *The Symbolism of the Christian Temple*, chaps. 3, 5, 12.

adheres harmoniously to the structure and the dynamic of the cosmos, the 'natural' manifestation of the Creative Divine Word.

These considerations induce us to see the metaphysical meaning of Christ's cross. The text from which to begin is that of St Paul: '. . . that ye, being rooted and grounded in love, may be able to comprehend with all saints what is the *breadth*, and *length*, and *depth*, and *height*; and know the love of Christ' (Eph. 3:17–18). All the Fathers have understood these lines with reference to the Cross, and more exactly to the extension of the cross to the universe. Recalling the famous passage from the *Timaeus* where Plato shows that the whole celestial vault turns about the great X formed by the plane of the equator and that of the ecliptic, they applied it to Christ, the constructive Logos of the world. Suspended from the 'cross that crucifies the world', He contains the cosmos and causes it to depend upon the mystery of that cross. Thus the cross 'recapitulates' the whole of cosmic becoming.

He who, through obedience to the cross, effaced on the wood the ancient disobedience, is Himself the Logos of God Almighty who penetrates all of us with an invisible presence, and this is why He embraces the entire world, its breadth and length, its height and depth. It is through the Logos of God that all things are conducted in an orderly way and the Son of God is crucified in them, whilst affixing His imprint to all in the form of the cross. It was therefore fitting and appropriate that when making Himself visible, He communicated to all that is visible His communion with all in the cross. For His action should show in visible things, and in a visible way, that it is He who illumines the heights, that is to say, heaven; who reaches right into the depths and foundations of the earth; who extends the surfaces from the east right to the west and spreads out the distances from the north even to the south, and from everywhere summons all that is scattered to know His Father.[24]

This text, which is very enlightening for our purpose, is from St Irenaeus who elsewhere says in a forceful formula in the same spirit:

24. St Irenaeus, *Demonstr.* 1, 34.

'Christ was nailed to the cross so as to there summarize the universe in Himself.'[25] This is echoed by St Andrew of Crete's hymn for the feast of the Exaltation of the Cross: 'O Cross, reconciliation of the cosmos, boundary of the expanses, depth of the earth and the height of heaven, bond of creation, extent of everything visible, breadth of the universe.'[26] The words 'extent of everything visible' are significant: Christ's crucifixion symbolizes the extending of the redemption to the whole cosmos.

But it is the symbolism of the tree that completes this symbolism. The cross is the Tree of Life, that very tree that was planted at the center of Eden and at the foot of which the source of the four rivers of Paradise gushed forth (Gen. 22:9–10). It is found again at the center of the Heavenly Jerusalem (Ezek. 47:12; Apoc. 2:7, 22:2) and Scripture identifies it with the Divine Wisdom and the Word (Prov. 3:18). The cross, the Tree of Life, substituted for that of Eden, is situated like it at the central point of the world. At the summit of Golgotha, the tree reached up towards heaven and embraced the world at the very place where, it is said, Adam was created and buried, such that the rivers of water and blood flowing from the Crucified One became the 'Fountain of Life' streaming over the body of the first man to raise him from among the dead.

The cosmic Tree, growing both vertically towards heaven and horizontally to the ends of the earth, is the figure of the extending of the redemption to the entire universe. Hippolytus of Rome has some wonderful words to say on this prodigy:

> This Tree, tall as the skies, was raised up to heaven from the earth. It is the solid support of everything, the point of repose of all things, the base of the world in its entirety, the cosmic polar point. In itself, it gathers into one all the diversity of human nature.... It reaches to the highest summits of heaven and with its feet supports the earth, and in its infinite arms it embraces the immense middle atmosphere that lies between the two.[27]

25. *Adv. Haeres.* 5, 18, 3.
26. *In sanct. Crucem.*
27. Hyppolytus of Rome, *Easter Homily*, 6.

A Greek commentator, Œcumenios of Trikka, explains the passage from St Paul concerning the four dimensions of the cross in the following way. The length is that the mystery of the cross has been foreseen from all eternity. The width is that all have benefited from it. The depth is that Christ has extended His blessings as far as Hell, while the height is that He who descended is also He who has re-ascended above all the powers (Eph. 4:9–10). We see that this is the whole mystery of salvation and its application to the world, to time and to space.

St Irenaeus' text shows us the importance of the central point of the cosmic cross, a point that is the heart of the world and the Heart of God simultaneously; this point is in fact where the vertical axis crosses the horizontal. It is the center of the world, the place where what is found on the terrestrial horizontal axis makes contact with the celestial realities of the vertical axis. The horizontal axis indicates the sense of 'amplitude', of the extension of the mystery even to the level of our world and our human state, its extension to all the ages and all the regions of the earth. The vertical axis indicates the sense of 'exaltation', of the ascent to higher states of Being, to heaven; this applies to the part of the axis situated above the horizontal. As for the part below, it represents inferior states of Being, the 'hells' in the widest sense—*inferi*—inferior states, obviously in relation to the human state.

The altar where the Divine Liturgy is celebrated is raised at precisely the central point of the cosmic cross, and, identified there with Christ Himself, as we have said, is the place where the human can meet the divine world. The vertical axis is the axis of redemption: Christ, who descended from Heaven to earth and as far as the depths of the lower regions, is 'risen to the heights, taking the captives with Him' (Psalm 67:18, 19, anthem of the Feast of the Ascension). The vertical branch of the cross determines the theanthropic trajectory. This is the path whereby God descends to man and man ascends to God, the way whereby Christ leads the world to the Father. As Supreme Pontiff, He raises the Church from earth to the heavenly assembly and the eternal liturgy described in the Epistle to the Hebrews and the Apocalypse.

Thus the cross determines the inner architecture of the mimodrama of the Mass, the axis of prayer and the axis of sacrifice. The axis of prayer, because, once again, if the whole structure we are studying is that of the cosmos, it is also that of the human body, constructed on a vertical axis governing its erect posture and height and corresponding to the polar axis, and a horizontal axis, determining its breadth. To which should be added, within the order of the dynamic of the body and the psyche, the importance of the verticalizing, ascensional pattern, specific to the human species, which is the psychosomatic source of all the images of ascension so important to our comportment and our appearance.[28] The most specific posture of prayer, that of the ancient way of praying, that of the priest during the celebration, is the upright position, with the eyes raised towards heaven and the arms extended horizontally; this posture reproduces exactly the figure of the cross. The vertical axis of the cross is also that of the sacrifice. We have already seen how, on several occasions, the priest *raises* the Holy Gifts and prays to the Lord to *lift them up* so as to transport them to the heavenly altar.

This dynamic of the offering corresponds to a fundamental and universal datum of the human psyche; we have encountered this gesture in ancient Egypt[29] and it would be easy to multiply examples, even in degenerate traditions like those of shamanism.[30] But we still have a magnificent specimen of it in the Mass in the form of the rite of censing. This rite, inherited from the Old Testament,[31] plays a threefold role: apotropaic, cathartic and sacrificial. In its apotropaic aspect, the priest's circumambulation of the altar is intended first and foremost to drive away the 'evil influences' for, always and everywhere, incense—or its equivalents—has had the

28. Regarding this, see G. Durand, *Les structures anthropologiques de l'imaginaire*, Paris, 1969.

29. Cf. above, p 64.

30. The Tongolese shaman carries the sacrifice to heaven; among the Yakuts, he uses for this rite a tree of nine ascending branches, which he climbs with the offering (M. Eliade, *Shamanism: Archaic Techniques of Ecstasy*, pp 118 and 275).

31. The High Priest could not begin the service without first censing (Lev. 16:12).

power to ward off demons.[32] The latter, we know, always have a tendency to come and lay siege to places where a sacred activity takes place. In its cathartic role, incense purifies from evil and sin: in the Syrian Mass, the priest beseeches God 'to accept the fragrance of this incense ... for our sins and shortcomings', and this, moreover, is one of the reasons for censing the faithful after the altar. Let us add that alongside this negative aspect there is a positive one. Certain essences, like incense in particular, reduced through burning to their most subtle elements, create a propitious milieu for receiving benefic influences; the blessings that descend during the celebration. And it is perhaps because of this that the perfume of the incense is considered as the 'sweet fragrance of Jesus Christ' which spreads from the altar into the souls of the faithful.[33] But there is more: the rite of censing constitutes a veritable *sacrifice,* and, returning to our subject, we would like to emphasize this point. Here too we find the archetype of the rite in the celestial liturgy of the Apocalypse: 'an angel came and stood at the altar of incense' (Apoc. 8:3), which is alluded to in the Roman Mass at the time of the censing in the offertory. In another passage we read that 'the elders fell down before the Lamb, having every one of them harps, and golden vials full of odors, which are the prayers of the saints' (Apoc. 5:8). In the offering of incense, the 'earthly' resin is sacrificed in a veritable holocaust: the material, its gross form abolished by the fire, becomes evanescent and its subtle essence rises to heaven. This is the sign of the sacrifice of the heart, which the Divine Fire needs must set alight. 'May the Lord,' says the officiant, 'light in us the fire of His Love and the flame of Eternal Charity'; and St Gregory the Great comments thus: 'The holy soul makes of its heart a censer that breathes forth its fragrances before God.'

The rite of censing falls within the same pattern of the Mass as a whole that we analyzed above. The censing is done according to

32. In the case of ancient Egypt, for example, cf. H. Bonnet, *Reallexikon d. aegypt. Religionsgeschichte,* p 624 ff. In the Brahmanic sacrifice, the priest with firebrand in hand circles the offering with the same apotropaïc intention (Goblet d'Alviella, *Croyances, rites, institutions,* 1911, vol. I, pp 8–9).

33. St Denis the Areopagyte, *Eccl. Hierarch,* 3 and 4. Symeon of Thessaloniki, *Concerning the Holy Temple.*

three figures: a circumambulation of the altar, a cruci-circular censing, and a vertical censing. We have already alluded to the circumambulation in speaking of the apotropaic role of the incense. This
ritual movement is not peculiar to the censing, for it is also done, at
least in the Byzantine rite, for the procession of the Gospel. Besides,
any procession is always more or less a circumambulation, either
around the temple, if on its outside, or around the altar if on the
inside. In both cases, it is a question of a movement about the center, the *omphalos*, which imitates that of the sun and of life around
the motionless axis of the world. The purpose of this ritual movement is to be imbued with the 'virtue' that emanates from the center and also cause it to radiate over the world.[34] The *cruci-circular
censing* obviously has the same goal in mind; it occurs at the time of
the offertory and before the circumambulation; although it is found
in all the rites, we shall describe it according to the Syrian ritual
where its import is much more apparent. The officiant first censes
the gifts in the form of a cross, and the rubrics specify that one is to
understand by this the dispatching of the incense to the four cardinal points in the following order: east, west, north, and south. He
then censes the gifts in the form of a circle. Thus the censing is done
according to a figure made up of a cross inscribed in a circle, which
we have seen above is the diagram of the universe. This figure is also
that of the terrestrial paradise and the cosmic mountain, with the
four oriented rivers symbolizing it. It is very significant that this figure be traced with the incense over the gifts placed on the altar, for
the altar represents Golgotha, and the Mountain of Zion with the
immolated Lamb whence flow the four rivers issuing from the
fountain of life, the image of Paradise regained, of the universe
regenerated. To our mind, there can be no doubt that the rite of
cruci-circular censing is an additional way of affirming and realizing the extending of redemption to the entire universe, an extension

34. Usually the circumambulations go from left to right, in the direction of the
sun's course. A delicate point, for what we are dealing with, is that the circumambulations of our liturgy are made in the opposite direction, towards the left, which
relates them to a polar orientation (this is known in Islam). Now, we scarcely see
any trace of polar orientation in the Christian liturgies.

symbolized by the Cross, whose four branches correspond to the cardinal points.[35] But, in another way, it is also a concentration, a synthetization of the universe led back, in its essential 'lines', to its divine center and marked with the sign of salvation. The world, gathered together in this way from the four horizons, is going to be offered, and thereby *raised* to heaven: this is the object of the third, vertical censing. It is done before the image of the crucifix, but that its sense surpasses that of a simple homage to the image of Christ is proved by the prayers accompanying it. The priest says: 'May this incense, blessed by Thee, Lord, *ascend* to Thee and may Thy mercy *descend* upon us. . . . May my prayer *ascend* to Thee like the smoke of incense in Thy presence, and my hands *lifted up*, like the evening sacrifice.' The column of rising smoke follows the direction of the axial pillar, which in a way it embodies, reaches the keystone of the vault, which it thus joins to the stone of the altar and, finally, symbolically passes beyond the vault to follow its course right to the summit of heaven—a fiery vehicle carrying prayer to the divine throne whence it brings blessings back to earth. *Incensum istud ascendat ad te et descendat super nos misericordia tua.*

The interpretation given here is in no way the fruit of our imagination, but is based upon a fundamental and universal pattern of the sacred. It has been demonstrated in a decisive fashion with regard to the Vedic sacrifice. There, the sacrificial smoke of the sacrifice is assimilated to the world axis. It conveys prayer up to the vault of the temple, to the eye of the dome, the opening which plays the same role as the key of the vault in our buildings and is identified with the gate of heaven, and then beyond the celestial vault; the souls of the officiant and the faithful rise along with it 'in the footsteps of Agni' (the Divine Fire), and in return heavenly grace descends to earth following the same axis.[36] The rite of the calumet, the principal rite of the Sioux Indians, falls within the same framework and is executed

35. The Syrian Jacobite ritual contains this prayer for the censing: 'The whole of creation is saturated with the fragrance of Thy divine sweetness. Grace is spread over all creatures.'

36. A. K. Coomaraswamy, *Janua Coeli* in *Zalmoxis*, II, 1939 (1941) [reprinted in Coomaraswamy, *The Door in the Sky* (Princeton, NJ: Princeton University Press, 1997), pp 60–61. ED].

according to the cruci-circular figure essential to their tradition. The bowl of the calumet is filled with pinches of an aromatic herb,[37] placed in relation to the directions of space, so as to symbolically concentrate the whole of creation there ('In this herb is the earth and all that inhabits it'). It is then offered to God ('We offer Him everything in the universe'). Man who, by summing up all creatures, occupies a central position in the world, is identified with the calumet and the embers. The latter transform the herb into smoke so as to send it to heaven, thereby announcing that everything created returns to God ('May the way of Thy people match that of this smoke').[38]

Thus, like the liturgical texts themselves, the rite of censing reveals that inner architecture of the Mass arranged around the cross, which, in its turn, reveals the full scope of the holy sacrifice. The latter is truly the spiritual integration of both the universe and man, and their transformation. According to the horizontal axis of the cross, the whole universe, summed up in the temple, and all men of every age, symbolized by the assembly of the faithful, are re-united around a center, the stone of the altar. This is the first phase of the Holy Mysteries: the passage from the circumference to the center, the 'gathering' of what was 'scattered'. On the altar stone, which is the point of intersection of the horizontal axis of the great cosmic cross with its vertical axis, the second phase of the Mysteries is realized. This is the assumption of the universe and man who, integrated in Christ, are raised up the axial pillar towards the 'gate of heaven', the key of the vault, pass through it, and attain the abode of the sun.

Parallel to what could be called this geometrical structure, we also discover in the Mass at least traces of a numerical one. This is not the place to enlarge upon the importance of number symbolism,

37. The ritual tobacco which, among these people, plays the same role as incense.
38. Black Elk, *The Sacred Pipe*, New York, 1971.

nor its basis. Neither do we intend a complete study of it in the Mass, but shall be content to point out the presence of principal significant numbers and reveal their value and role in the Divine Liturgy wherever they appear.

First of all the number *three.* It is very apparent in the *Kyrie,* the *Agnus Dei,* and the *mea culpa* of the *Confiteor.* But it also appears, albeit in a more discrete way in the prayers at the foot of the altar: the verse of Psalm 42, *Introibo ad altare Dei,* is repeated three times. Let us add the three signs of the cross that are traced on the face before the reading of the gospel and that the priest makes at different times over the Holy Gifts: at the *Te igitur,* for example, the *Per quem omnia* and the *Pax Domini* (the breaking of the host). Three is the trinitarian and creative number, and there is no need to insist much upon the importance of its presence in the Mass, which is celebrated to the glory of the Holy Trinity, the three Persons of which are constantly invoked at the end of all prayers. In the *Kyrie,* the number 3, repeated in a triple ternary, gives the number *nine,* which is its square. *Nine* is the expression of a complete development. In effect, *three* is the creative number, and its square designates the multiple creation and announces its passage to the number *ten,* which is fullness. This is why the choirs of Angels, who are the spiritual creation, are nine in number. Thus the triple ternary of the *Kyrie* while glorifying the Trinity, further expresses, as a variation, its overflowing into creation.

Five rules a certain number of sequences, the most conspicuous being the five signs of the cross that in the Roman Canon accompany the prayer *Quam oblationem* and the great proclamation ending it: *Per Ipsum, cum Ipso et in Ipso.* The number *five* is the sign of life in the world, of animation and, as is well known, the sign of man. In the prayer *Quam oblationem,* just before the consecration, the five signs of the cross, that is five benedictions, are the announcement of the passage that is going to be effected for the Gifts from inert matter to life, and what life! In the proclamation *Per Ipsum,* etc., the five signs of the cross announce that He who is Himself called the Life (*Ego sum via, lux et vita*) is now present on the altar to reconcile everything in heaven and on earth; He the Man-God.

The number *seven*, whose sacred symbolism is known to all (the seven days of Creation, the seven gifts of the Holy Spirit, the seven spirits before the Throne of God in the Apocalypse, etc.),[39] is according to St Augustine[40] the sign of perfection and fullness. It rules not only the lights, as we have seen, but the greetings of the priest to the congregation: he pronounces *Dominus vobiscum* seven times. In fact, what greater fullness of perfection could one desire than the one that is born when indeed 'the Lord is with us'?

Between the ascension to the altar and the final benediction, the priest kisses the altar *eight* times. We have explained the meaning of this kiss: it is the symbol of the nuptial union of the Church with Christ.[41] Now the meaning of the number *eight* confirms this symbolism. According to St Augustine, it is the number of the resurrection,[42] for it designates the union of man, 5, with the Creator, 3, which in fact is fully realized in Christ, and, by way of consequence, among His faithful followers. This is why in the first centuries the baptistery, where this resurrection of man takes place, was often octagonal in shape.[43]

All traditions have accorded a great importance to the number *ten*, the Decade. It is the symbol of totality, or the universe; it is in fact viewed as composite unity, *One* being synthetic unity; the *One* is the First Cause, *ten* the total effect, the reflection of the Cause. In the Roman Mass, the company of saints is mentioned ten times to recall that the Divine Liturgy is the work through which the integration of the entire Church is effected. *Ten* is found again, but in a hidden form, in the chant of the *Sanctus*, which is an integration of the universe.[44]

The number *twelve* evokes somewhat the same reality in the Mass. It is, in itself, the number of cosmic functioning ruled by the twelve signs of the Zodiac, whence the twelve months of the year. But the signs of the Zodiac and the months have been related to the

---

39. Cf. above, p89.
40. *Quaest*. 42; *In Heptat*. 5, 42. Cf. Tertullian, *De anima*, 37.
41. Cf. above, pp76–77.
42. St Augustine, *Epist*. 56.
43. See our *Symbolism of the Christian Temple*, p67.
44. Cf. below, pp130–133.

twelve tribes of Israel and the twelve Apostles:[45] like the signs around the visible sun, the Apostles surround Jesus, the 'Sun of Righteousness'. In the Canon of the Roman Mass, following the Remembrance of the Living, the celebrant, in the prayer *Communicantes*, cites the twelve Apostles after the Most Holy Virgin, adding to them the names of twelve martyrs of the Roman Church. In this way he obtains the number twenty-four, which is that of the Elders of the Apocalypse (4:4), which means that he and with him the whole congregation is united to the Church Triumphant.[46]

In the last prayer of the Canon, *Nobis quoque peccatoribus*, which develops the same theme, the priest cites fifteen names of Apostles and Martyrs. The number *fifteen* plays an important role in Christian symbolism. According to St Jerome, it is the fullness of knowledge and according to St Augustine, the union of the two Testaments: 7, the Sabbath, and 8, the Resurrection.[47] Let us also recall the 15 mysteries of the Virgin in the Rosary and its fifteen decades, about which we shall speak in a moment. Finally, let us note that fifteen is the number of the Divine Name *Yah*, which we encountered in the acclamation *Alleluia*, and which is an abridgment of the Tetragram YHWH. *Yah* is written with the two consonants YH, since in Hebrew the vowels are not properly speaking written; now, $H = 5$ and $Y = 10$. This union of the Y and the H, say the Jews, gives birth to the Heavenly River, which is like the flowing of Divinity into cosmic manifestation.

The prayers at the foot of the altar comprise *seventeen* prayers or invocations. The *Gloria*, for its part, is made up of *seventeen* verses. In light of this, we need to pause here, for the number 17 is one of the most important and mysterious in Christianity, and it is doubtless not without reason that one finds it inserted twice in the course of the Mass. *Seventeen* is the eighth prime number. If one triangulates it, that is to say adds up the sequence of numbers from 1–17, one gets

45. St Augustine, *In Ps.* 103, 3.

46. See our *Symbolism of the Christian Temple*, p76 and 131ff. Cf. J. Daniélou, *Primitive Christian Symbols*, Baltimore, 1964, p124 ff.

47. St Jerome, *In Gal.* 1, 1; St Augustine, *In Ps.*, 89, 10; 150, 1. Cf. St Hilary, *In Ps.* 118. St Ambrose, *Epist.* 44.

153.[48] Now it is in connection with the second miraculous catch of fish that 153 is mentioned by St John (21:1–14) who tells us that the apostles, having thrown the nets into the sea, drew in a large catch comprising 153 fish. It would be absolutely astonishing if the Evangelist went to the trouble of such precision, in connection with a catch, if this precision did not contain some secret message for us. It is to St Augustine that the honor is due for having deciphered the passage from verse 11 of St John. He started from the number 17 considered as 10 + 7. Ten is the Law (the Decalogue) and 7 is the Holy Spirit with His seven gifts called the 7 'Spirits of God'; the number 17 signifies that the Holy Spirit, sent by Christ, is added to the Law (7 + 10) and that thus the 'Spirit' quickens the 'letter'. Then St Augustine triangulated 17 and thereby came to the 153 of St John, which he interpreted as follows: 153 is the symbolic number of saints who live from the Spirit of God in accordance with the Law. In effect, 153 = (50 x 3) + 3; three is the Trinity and 50 = (7 x 7) + 1, which is the Gifts of the Holy Spirit squared, that is to say spread over individuals, plus 1, to remind us that the Spirit is *one* despite the multiplicity of its actions. At the same time, 50 corresponds to the Holy Spirit from the fact that it was sent on the 50th day after the Resurrection. Thus, concluded St Augustine, the miraculous catch of the 153 fish is the sign of the regeneration of men through the quickening of the letter of the Law, 10, by the Spirit of Jesus, 7.[49] To conclude, let us add that through reduction, 17 = 1 + 7 = 8, which, we have seen, is also a Christic number par excellence, being that of the Resurrection. In the *Gloria*, with its 17 verses, there are 8 for the Father, 8 for the Son and 1 for the Holy Spirit. One has then 8 + 8 + 1 = 17, while on the other hand, 17 = 7 + 1 = 8. If one places these two calculations next to each other, one obtains the figure 8 three times; now 888 is the number of the Name of Jesus in Greek, as already mentioned.[50]

---

48. One obtains the triangular value by means of the formula $\frac{n(n+1)}{2}$; in the case in question $\frac{17(17+1)}{2} = 153$.

49. St Augustine, *122nd Treatise on St John*. Notice that the Rosary is made up of 15 decades, that is 150 *Aves* to which it is necessary to add the three preliminary *Aves*, which gives a total of 153. This is certainly not fortuitous.

50. IHCOYC: I (10) + H (8) + C (200) + O (70) + Y (400) + C (200) = 888.

During the course of the Roman Mass the celebrant makes the sign of the cross *thirty-three* times. This number is not a matter of chance; it is full of meanings that we cannot go into here. Let us simply recall, on the one hand, that Christ lived for 33 years, which corresponds perfectly with the performance of the Mass, which is the Act of Christ Himself, while on the other hand 33 governs the whole structure of the *Divine Comedy* whose mystical meaning is well known.

We shall end this quick review of the numerical harmonics of the Mass with the most beautiful, that of the *Lord's Prayer*, which is magnificently constructed according to a septenary structure. In effect, the Lord's Prayer comprises seven requests, divided into three requests concerning God and four concerning man. Now, the number 3, we have already said, is that of the divine world, and 4, that of the terrestrial world. One understands then the full value of the 'rhythm' given to the prayer through this numerical harmonic of $3 + 4 = 7$, which is that of Creation itself according to Genesis. On the other hand, this structure corresponds directly to the seven Christian virtues, which are comprised of the three theological virtues and the four cardinal virtues, the first corresponding to the divine world and the second to the human and earthly domain:

> Our Father, which art in heaven,
>   hallowed be Thy Name;   [*Faith*]
> 3 Thy Kingdom come;   [*Hope*]
> Thy will be done on earth,
>   as it is in heaven;   [*Charity*]

> Give us this day our daily bread; [*Strength*]
>   and forgive us our trespasses
> 4   as we forgive those who trespass against us; [*Justice*]
>   and lead us not into temptation, [*Prudence*]
>   but deliver us from evil. [*Temperance*]

Another altogether interesting correspondence is that which derives from the geometric construction corresponding to 7, namely a triangle, 3, symbol of the divine, over a square, 4, symbol of the earth. This figure represents the section of the 'pointed cubic stone', the symbolic piece that played a major role in the artisanal organizations of builders. We cannot enlarge upon this subject here. It is easy, however, to understand this figure's message; the square of the cardinal virtues, solidly established and unshakable, is the indispensable base and support enabling the individual to ascend to the triangle that points towards heaven, that is to say enter the divine world by way of the three theological virtues. Thus, through its numerical structure, the Lord's Prayer reveals to us that it is the perfect act of piety summing up the whole process of sanctification and salvation.[51]

51. A pointed cubic stone is made up of a pyramid surmounting a cube. The pyramid being related to the *tetraktys* (the sequence of the numbers 1, 2, 3, 4), and the traditional cube of this stone having 4 sides, it has been noticed that the value derived from the *tetraktys* suspended over the square of 4 sides gives $1+2+3+4=10$ and $4\times4=16$, that is to say 26. Now 26 is the number of the Great Divine Name YHWH.

5

Dramatis Personae

WITHIN the vast scene constituted by the temple, the altar is the pole of attraction, around which the actors in the mimodrama of the Mass revolve, speak and act.

These actors form a whole, the *synaxis*, that is to say the assembly, the assembly of Christians. The latter is hierarchic, in the sense that at its head is the priest. In this position he plays a pre-eminent role, as much from a theological as from what could be called a dramatic point of view, as consecrator, and because he, with the deacon, directs the dramatic play of the sacrifice.[1] It is important, however, to specify immediately that he is not the only actor in the liturgy, as too many people still believe in spite of the teaching of the Church. To understand the meaning and scope of the Mass, one needs to see clearly the precise role of the respective players in it.

Because he takes the place of Christ Himself in the Divine Liturgy, the priest is incontestably the principal actor. In fact, the true and only actor is Christ, at the same time Priest and Victim of the sacrifice, as all orthodox theology teaches. But through the very wish of Christ, clearly expressed at the Last Supper of Maundy Thursday, He is represented by and visibly acts through the man who is vested with His own priesthood.

During the celebration, the reading of the Scripture and, still more, the eucharistic anaphora, the priest is completely identified with Christ. And here once again, we state that this cultic and theological truth of Christianity corresponds to a universal reality of the sacred. In all traditions we find numerous rites in which the links

---

1. It goes without saying, but nevertheless we recall it, that if the Mass unfolds like a scenic play, it is not, as was specified above, theater, pp 54–55.

between the officiant and the god are very close. We have already cited the case of Egypt where the priests represent the gods Horus and Seth.[2] It is very often the case that the priest wears the dress or mask of the god[3] or bears his name[4] or, in a word, appears as his total incarnation. Thus in the Dionysian mysteries, the leader of the ritual dance was identified completely with Dionysius.[5] This investing of the priest by the god answers to a profound and double need in man: the need, first of all, to be sure of the efficacy of the rite— now, only the god, in one way or another, has the power to render it efficacious—and the need, subsequently, of the effective presence, direct or indirect, of the god made, so to say, tangible.

One of the most sensible signs of the sacred character of the officiant is his dress. We would like to insist somewhat upon this matter, first of all because the officiant is an actor, and an actor's costume is not something negligible. Secondly, because there is currently in the church of the West a tendency to minimize the importance of this accessory or even to eliminate it from the cult. In this there is grave danger for reasons we shall to try to explain.

Is there need to say that the wearing of special vestments for the celebration of the Mass is an absolutely strict rule of the Church, from which one cannot deviate, except in cases of absolute necessity, perforce very rare? In order to dispense with it, it is altogether vain to invoke here the fact that, at the beginning of Christianity, the priests celebrated the Mass in the costume of everyday life. If they did, this was precisely for the reasons just pointed out: insecurity created by persecutions, the absence, most of the time, of proper places of worship, and the need to celebrate, so to say, clandestinely. Of this we are quite certain. Also, consideration should perhaps be given to locale, because we know, moreover, that St John, to celebrate the Divine Liturgy, wore a sort of gold ring on his forehead, in imitation of the Hebrew high priest. One can infer from this that

2. See p 69, n 27.
3. O. Gruppe, *Griech. Mythologie*, II, p 924.
4. Frazer, *Golden Bough*. I, p 300.
5. *Ibid.*, I, pp 286, 343, 368, 370; II, pp 2, 27. Among the Dogons, the priest of Nommo, during his consecration, is totally identified with Nommo; see M. Griaule, *Dieu d'eau*, 1966, p 114.

this was not the only cultic vestment he possessed and that he put on special clothes. What is more, one should not forget that the ordinary dress of antiquity was not, like that of our age, totally profane. It had a certain sacred character, as we shall perhaps have occasion to say, such that to celebrate the Mass in a toga, at Rome or Milan for example, had nothing in common with the fact of saying it in a full lounge suit. In any case, from the time that the cult could be freely and openly organized and celebrated, special vestments were used. This is proved by a passage from St Jerome saying 'one should not enter the Holy of Holies and celebrate the sacraments of the Lord in the clothes that serve us in the other walks of life. . . . Divine religion has a dress for the ministry and another for common use.'[6] True, civic garments were retained, but they would be transformed, over and above being blessed, by the addition of Christic signs, and in the first instance with crosses.

This rule can only be understood properly by starting from an exact knowledge of the true nature and use of clothing, a knowledge that has unfortunately become thoroughly strange to the modern mentality. In traditional societies great importance is attached to clothing and there are precise rules regarding its form, decoration, and use, rules deriving from a true science of dress, itself dependent more or less directly, like all science, on metaphysical principles. In every way, even outside of a special science that may be applicable to it, clothing presents fundamental, easily recognized characteristics if we but reflect on this a moment.

First of all it is the outer sign of the personality wearing it and more especially of his position in society: it exteriorizes and manifests the individual's function. This, to a certain degree, more or less, is still true even in the modern world: the soldier, the lawyer, the judge, the religious, the king, each wear a uniform that points to the role he plays. But it is not simply a sign; the influence of the uniform is exerted in a much wider domain; in expressing the function it comes to influence, to complete or change the personality. If a French proverb has it that 'the habit does not make the monk', there exists a German proverb that says exactly the opposite: *Kleider*

---

6. St Jerome, *In Ezech.*, 44.

machen Leute, 'clothes maketh the man'; which is not at all untrue. Everyone can observe how wearing a particular garment modifies one's comportment. This is because the self tends to be effaced before the function, such that we are in a way remodeled by the clothing. And this also is true, in a less precise but similar way, perhaps, for garments that are not properly speaking uniforms. The choice of a particular garment, its color and embellishments, reveal the soul, the character of its owner. In a spectacular way, the Indian *sari*, for example, truly reveals the soul of the race.

In all religions, the case of the priest is even clearer. More than before any other function, the man who dons the clothes of an officiant effaces himself—because he needs to be effaced—before the priestly function. The sacerdotal vestment 'sacrifices' the officiant, in both senses of the word: it in a way effaces the individual but on the other hand, confers a sacred character upon the person, for he is conceived as the visible sign of the religious or divine principle of the priesthood. Whence all the details of form, color and ornamentation aimed at specifying the different aspects of this principle.

The same goes for the sacerdotal clothes of the Christian priest. But to tell the truth, it is not only they that are of concern: the question of clothing is of interest to all Christians, they being marked, moreover, with a certain priestly character, as we shall soon see.

The conception of clothing in Christianity is based on the one hand on the passage from Genesis, reporting the state of man after the fall, and on the other, on the Pauline doctrine of the 'new man'. In Paradise Adam was clothed with a garment of light, which was the 'glory' that irradiated his body, the reflection of the Glory of God Himself.[7] Through his sin, he was stripped of it and, 'seeing he was naked', concocted 'habits of fig leaves' for himself and Eve (Gen. 3:6 ff.). God subsequently gave them 'tunics of skin' (Gen. 3:21). But the Christ of the Transfiguration and the Resurrection restored his garments of glory to man: this is the 'robe of immortality' (*endyma aftharsias*),[8] which is Christ Himself according to St Paul:

7. St Irenaeus, *Adv haeres*, 3, 23, 5; St John Chrysostom, *In Gen.* 16, 5; St Gregory of Nyssa, *De virginit.*, 3.

8. St Gregory of Nyssa, *Hom. baptism.* PG 46, 420c.

'You have put on Christ' (Gal. 3:27). This is the work of baptism where we receive the robe of immortality, which, according to the forceful expression of the Syrian Liturgy, 'is woven of the water of baptism.'[9] This formula is magnificently illustrated in the traditional icon of the Baptism of Jesus, which shows the waters of Jordan descending vertically upon the body of the standing Lord and enveloping it like a cloak. The symbol of this garment of glory is the white robe of the newly baptized. At baptism man takes off the clothes of the 'old man', the 'garment of fig leaves' and the 'tunic of skin', and can sing out, 'The Lord has renewed me with His garment and clothed me with light.'[10] This is the wedding garment that makes us worthy to enter the banquet (Matt. 22:11). And this is why, in the Roman rite, the priest says to the recipient, 'Receive this white garment, intending to wear it intact before the judgment seat of Our Lord Jesus Christ so as to have eternal life.'

This white robe is the specific garment of the Christian, be he layman or priest. In the case of the priest, it is the *alb*, a tunic of white linen (*Alba vestis*), being the first garment he puts on before celebrating. But, over and above each one's particular symbolism, it is an ensemble of vestments, the amice, stole, and chasuble, which is traditionally assimilated to the 'garment of glory' of regenerated man. Vesting prayers in the Armenian rite are particularly instructive in this regard. The priest recites the following prayer: 'O Jesus Christ, Our Lord, who is clothed in splendor as with a dazzling garment . . . .[11] O Lord cause thy light to clothe me. . . .' At the same time the choir chants:

O Profound Mystery! O Incomprehensible! Above us Thou hast adorned the Principalities with an inaccessible light, and clothed

9. Sachau, *Syrische Rechtsbücher*, II, p9.

10. *Odes of Solomon*, 12. Cf. a sedro [a prayer of reconciliation] of the matins prayer for the Sunday before Christmas: 'Today we have taken off our garments of shame that have clothed us since the beginning, habits of fig leaves, and adorned ourselves with garments of splendor, glory, and beauty' (*L'Orient Syrien*, Vol. 1, 1956, p93).

11. The Lord reigneth, he is clothed with majesty; the Lord is clothed with strength' (Psalm 92). 'O Lord my God, thou art very great; thou art clothed with honor and majesty. Who coverest thyself with light as with a garment' (Psalm 103).

the angels with a transcendent glory.... Through the Passion of Thine only Son all creatures shall be renewed and within the New Man shall become immortal and be adorned with a garment of which nothing shall be able to despoil them.

The beauty of the sacerdotal vestments, the richness of the silks, the splendor of the fabrics and of the gold embroidery, even sometimes the precious stones set in them, the purpose of all this is to embody and symbolize, for our eyes of flesh, that transcendent light that emanates from God and envelopes creatures, and more especially he who incarnates God Himself during the sacrifice. This is why the priest, clothed in full regalia is an object of contemplation for the congregation, what in India is called *darshan*. By simply *gazing*, and benefiting from the *darshan* of this personage, one is penetrated with the imponderables of his appearance and with the symbolism proceeding from his sacred costume. Virgil Gheorgiu recounts that the first image to strike him in childhood was that of his father clothed in priestly garments to celebrate the Divine Liturgy:

My father clothed in vestments of gold and silver no longer had anything earthly or worldly about him. The sacerdotal vestments signify that the priest has completely cut all his attachments with the world and is the personification of God.[12]

And, in another passage, he writes that his father resembled an icon.[13] This was truly the case, for an icon is an object of contemplation in that it reveals the invisible reality in a visible way. This impression is particularly palpable in the cultic appearance of the Byzantine or Armenian priest. Draped in rich white, gold or silver silks with the tiara surmounted by the cross on his head, he is truly like an earthly hypostasis of the Eternal Priest draped in the splendor of the Divine Light.

It is out of the question to give a full account here of the sacerdotal vestments; it would not only take too long, but is also beyond the

12. Reference to St Simeon of Thessalonika, *On the Holy Liturgy*, 79.
13. Virgil Gheorgiu, *De la vingt-cinquième heure à l'heure éternelle*, pp 61–62 and pp 8–9.

bounds of our study. We would like nevertheless to bring to light certain aspects of the matter, which will allow for a better understanding of the spirit of the Divine Liturgy.

Over his usual clothes the priest, as already mentioned, puts on the *alb*, the tunic of white linen symbolizing purity, which replaces the 'tunic of skin' and the 'garment of fig leaves'. Already, among the Jews, the high priest could not enter the sanctuary without first putting on a robe of linen (Lev. 16). In the Apocalypse (7:13–14), this is the robe of the elect, which allows one to approach the Lamb. In addition, while putting it on the priest recites this prayer: 'Make me white, O Lord, and purify my heart, so that, being made white in the Blood of the Lamb, I may deserve an eternal reward.'[14] The Latin priest next places over his head, then flattens around his neck, a cloth called the *amice*, the purpose of which among the ancient Romans was purely utilitarian, but which has taken on a spiritual meaning in the liturgy, as indicated by the prayer that is recited. 'Place, O Lord, the helmet of salvation upon my head to resist the attacks of the devil.' The image of the helmet comes from St Paul who, in the Epistle to the Ephesians (6:13–17), enumerates the spiritual arms the Christian ought to possess to struggle against the Devil. The amice has therefore an apotropaïc role, as does the *cincture* or *cord* with which the priest girds himself over the alb. The prayer he recites shows that this belt completes the role of the alb. 'Gird me, O Lord, with the cincture of purity and extinguish in my heart the fire of concupiscence so that, the virtue of continence and chastity always abiding in my heart, I may the better serve Thee.'

We cannot miss raising here the objection of certain modern liturgists who consider the symbolism of the vestments we have mentioned, and of others we shall cite in due course, to be artificial. According to them, prior to being used in the liturgy, these vestments had no spiritual meaning, this having been attached to them in a wholly conventional way. To which we reply, once more, that true symbolism is never conventional—like the emblem or allegory—but is connatural with the object, resulting from its form,

---

14. The white robes of the heavenly beings signify the divine form in relation to fire and light, according to Denis the Areopagite, *Cel. Hier.* 15, 4.

color, and material, etc. The symbolism may be, moreover, only latent with several possible meanings. This is explained quite naturally when integrated, as we saw above, into a structural whole, which allows a certain aspect of the symbolism to fully reveal itself on being inserted into the determining patterns of the structure in question, in this case the liturgy of the Mass.

Leaving aside the symbolism of the alb, which no one contests since it is based on Scripture itself, let us speak of that of the amice and cincture, which, although less obvious at first sight, is nevertheless as real. As soon as the amice is placed on the head, it falls within the general category of head-dresses, of which the symbolism is multiple and of which the helmet is a special type, as the protective head-gear for combat; whence one passes quite naturally to the idea of spiritual combat. As for the cincture, it falls within the well-known category of protective circles, in which capacity it plays both an inner and outer role vis-à-vis the celebrant. First of all it constitutes a closed circuit against the evil and 'wandering influences' about which we have already spoken in saying that they particularly seek, during sacred activities, to lay siege to the places and persons involved. In this respect the cincture plays, vis-à-vis the celebrant, a similar role to that of the circle traced around the altar with incense. Furthermore, placed as a belt around the body, it separates—at the level of the navel, which is the center of the vertical symmetry of man—the lower parts of the physical and subtle organism, which is the seat of the animal passions, from the upper part, the heart and head, which alone should act during the liturgy. This is the explanation of the terms of the prayer recited while one puts it on.[15]

Two vestments altogether specific to the priest are the *stole* and the *chasuble*.

The word *stole* comes from the Greek (*stoli*) via the Latin (*stola*). In antiquity it designated a long vestment open in front and deco-

---

15. Speaking of the representations of the bodiless beings of heaven, St Denis writes with regard to their belts: 'They signify the care with which they conserve their generative powers; the power they have to recollect themselves, to concentrate their mental powers by entering into themselves, by folding up harmoniously upon themselves within the indefectible circle of their own identity' (*Cel. Hier.*, 15, 4).

rated on each side of the opening with two vertical bands of precious cloth. According to most historians, the modern stole derived from these two bands, which were 'detached' from the rest of the costume. But according to others, the stole came from the *ephod* of the Hebrew high priest, a scarf the tails of which were held together by a fibula over the chest, as currently the tails of the stole are joined by a small cord. There are some monuments of the first centuries showing Sts Peter and Paul with this vestment.[16] Be that as it may, the stole is the very insignia of the priesthood and the wearing of it is obligatory for all sacred activity. Like the alb, it is assimilated to the robe of innocence. When putting it on, the priest says: 'Restore unto me, O Lord, the stole of immortality which I lost through the sin of my first parents and, although unworthy to approach Thy sacred Mystery, may I nevertheless attain to joy eternal.' The stole is always marked with two crosses among the Latins and seven among the Greeks, like the Latin pallium.

The *chasuble*, which comes from the Latin *casula*, meaning 'small house', is made of a round piece of cloth, pierced in the middle with a hole for the head to pass through and falling down to just above the ankle. Such is the true chasuble, a magnificent garment, quite different from that ridiculous vestment called the Roman chasuble, made from a rectangle of stiff material at the back and a sort of figure cut out in the shape of a violin for the front of the body. Such an item of clothing no longer has anything garment-like or natural about it, and consequently loses all true meaning. Happily, it is disappearing more and more in favor of the so-called 'Gothic' chasuble, that is to say the chasuble as it has existed from the beginning. The vesting prayer for the chasuble, in the Latin rite, applies to it a symbolism derived from those previously mentioned artificial meanings.[17] The true symbolism of the chasuble is given by the cross, the initials of Christ: I H C, or the Chrismon, which are drawn on the back, signifying that the chasuble clothes the celebrant with a new personality, that of Christ. Originally, it was not a cross that

---

16. R. Gilles, *Le symbolisme dans l'art religieux*, Paris, Ed. Guy Tredaniel, p 55.

17. 'O Lord, Who hast said, "My yoke is sweet and My burden light," grant that I may so carry it as to merit Thy grace.'

was represented, but two bands of material of a different color from that of the habit itself, which descended from the shoulders and joined a central band. During the Gothic era the central band was extended upwards making of it a forked cross. Undoubtedly research should be pursued into the meaning of this design which, in its two forms, might well be related to the tree of the *sephiroth*, the subtle constitution of man and the doctrine of Universal Man.[18]

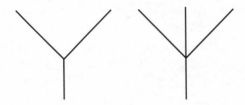

Their *color* completes the general symbolism of the sacerdotal vestments. On this point, too, we shall be brief, because the very important question of colors, in order to be properly explained, would need to be gone into in far too much depth. Let us say simply that the symbolism of color is one of the most important, because it is connected to that of light, which is probably the most adequate symbol of the Divinity. Colors are in fact only differentiations of light, as the whole world knows through the elementary experience of the spectrum and the phenomenon of the rainbow. Essentially the seven natural colors are like the deployment of white light, into which they are reabsorbed, just as all numbers proceed from unity and return to it.

The colors used in the liturgy are white, red, yellow, blue, green, violet and black.

Basically, *white* is the absence of color through an excess of light. It is the symbol of Being and Absolute Truth. In the Transfiguration

---

18. What is interesting is that the two upper bands start from the shoulders in the form of a St Andrew's cross: if the head of the celebrant corresponds to Kether, the two bands will correspond to Hokhmah and Bina, their point of juncture being in Tiphereth; the central band will join Tiphereth to Kether above, and to Yesod and Malkuth below.

on Tabor, Jesus appeared with garments dazzling like white wool and snow. It is the symbol of the Divine Unity and, for man, of the soul united with the Divinity, regenerated and pure. Up to the fourth century only white vestments were used in worship. Subsequently *red* was added, the symbol of fire, of Divine Love and the Holy Spirit as the fire of that love regenerating mankind. Red vestments were used for the feasts of the Holy Spirit, and those of the martyrs, not so much because of the color of blood as because of the love they proved through their sacrifice, love inspired certainly by the Holy Spirit.

Yellow is the color of *gold*. It is the revelation of the love and wisdom of God, transmitted by the Light, the Word, because, subtly, 'alchemically', yellow is produced by 'red' (Love) and 'white' (Wisdom). Vestments in cloth of gold, which could take the place of those of other colors, except black and violet, signified this revelation of God transmitted by the Light.

Blue, which is no longer used in the western Church, is a specific symbol of the Spirit, of the Holy Spirit, no longer considered as devouring Fire, but as breath, air (the blue of heaven) and as wisdom. In the icon of Christ, the Saviour is sometimes clothed with two robes, one red and one blue. These two colors are the two aspects of the Holy Spirit, the 'Spirit of Jesus'.

Green, the synthesis of yellow and blue, symbolizes the action resulting from creation through the Wisdom and Love of God and from the revelation of these divine virtues to the human intelligence through the Breath, the Pneuma. It is also equally the symbol of regeneration, and of life. Green vestments are used between Epiphany and Septuagesima, then from the third Sunday after Pentecost until Advent. This is because these times recall the two great events of the life of the world: natural life through creation and the life of Grace through the Resurrection of Christ, whence hope (green is the color of hope, of immortality).

Violet, derived from red and blue, that is to say the love of truth and the truth of love, marks the union of these two colors. It is also interpreted as coming from red and black: it then symbolizes penitence, which is an act of sorrowful suffering (black) and an act of love (red) in the motivation that spurs us on to suffer.

Black, the negation of light, generally has a pejorative meaning. But in the liturgy it is simply a sign of mourning in an outward sense, and, more inwardly, of the preliminary step to the resurrection, 'the black work'; the Holy Saturday prelude to the resurrection of Christ. It is put on at funerals of the faithful, their death being but the necessary passage to another life.

All these symbols, forms, and colors, harmoniously combined, contribute to create a propitious ambiance for sacred activity.

What we have just said suffices to show that the priest is the principal actor in the mimodrama of the Mass. But he is not the only one; all the faithful are also actors in it. This is why expressions such as 'to hear Mass' or 'attend Mass' are totally inadequate to the extent that they leave one to believe that the layman's role there is purely passive. It needs to be said that a certain attitude of the clergy, which has established itself in the western Church, has contributed to the spread this opinion. Forced by the Protestant Reformation, which suppressed the sacerdotal ministry and thereby destroyed the Mass, the Church forcefully recalled, and rightly so, the specific role of the priest. But the counter-thrust, if we may use this familiar turn of phrase, subsequently over-reached, practically causing the existence of the 'priesthood of the faithful' to be forgotten. And it is truly astonishing that many Christians, still faithful to tradition, seem determined to ignore this reality, which has its foundation in Scripture. It was St Peter himself, in his first epistle, who said of the whole Church that it was a 'kingdom of priests', that the disciples of Christ received a 'royal priesthood' (1 Pet. 2:9). Now, the passage from this letter is read on the Saturday after Easter, in connection with the newly baptized, which is quite remarkable, for thereby the priesthood of all Christians is announced to those who have just entered the Church. This truth has been constantly affirmed in the tradition since the Apostles. St Irenaeus said: 'It is we, as the priest, who offer';[19] and St John Chrysostom when speaking of the beginning of the Canon with the *Sursum corda* and what follows: 'It is not

19. *Adv. haer.* 4, 17, 18.

the priest alone who celebrates the thanksgiving (= the eucharist), but the people with him.'[20] Lastly we shall refer to the Papal Encyclicals: 'The sacrifice of the New Covenant constitutes ... that perfect homage in which the principal sacrificer, Christ, and with and through Him, all his mystical members, glorify God by rendering Him due homage' (Pius XII, *Mediator Dei*); 'in becoming 'sons of God' (John 1:12), adopted sons (Rom. 8:23), we at the same time become in His likeness 'a kingdom of priests', we receive the 'royal priesthood' (1 Pet. 2:9, Apoc. 5:10), that is to say, we participate in that unique and irreversible restitution of man and the world to the Father, which He, both eternal Son and true man, accomplished once for all' (John Paul II, *Redemptor hominis*).

Thus, one should not be afraid, with an archpriest of the Byzantine rite, to say out loud that 'the faithful concelebrate with the priest'. Besides, the texts themselves of the liturgy exhort us to it; the Roman Mass even seems to want to insist upon it; thus, before starting the Canon, the priest, facing the congregation, says, 'Pray, brethren, that *my sacrifice and yours* may become acceptable to God the Father almighty'; in the course of the canon, before the Consecration: 'Be mindful, O Lord, of Thy servants ... on whose behalf we offer unto Thee, or who *themselves offer unto Thee, this sacrifice* of praise for themselves and all their own....' 'Graciously accept, then... this service of our worship and that of all Thy household.' After the Consecration: 'Mindful, therefore, O Lord ... of the blessed passion of the same Christ ... we, Thy ministers, as also Thy holy people, offer unto Thy supreme majesty ... the pure Victim....' By way of these texts we see that it is not, as is often repeated, only through the hymns of praise and the acclamations of the Preparation, and at the moment of the Offertory that the people participate in the Liturgy: they are participants in the sacrifice properly so-called.

20. *In II Cor. Hom.* 18 (PG 61, 527). And from another witness, Gregory of Tours: *(mulier) celebrans quotidie missarum sollemnia et offerens oblationem pro memoria viri sui.* Cf. St Augustine: 'The word priest does not only include bishops and priests, who are properly priests of the Church, but also all of the Christians, on account of the mystical anointing which makes them members of the one and only priest, Jesus Christ' (*Civ. Dei*, 17, 4).

In order to understand things properly, one needs to remember that it is the *ecclesia*, or holy assembly, that is the subject of the Divine Liturgy. Christ transmitted His priesthood to the Universal Church, to the end that, through the ministry of the priests, it might accomplish the mystical immolation: the Church, that is, *all* the faithful, the Mystical Body. Symbolically, the local congregation, the *synaxis*, represents the Church and, in this capacity, it offers the sacrifice. Most assuredly, it is a hierarchically structured assembly, and it offers *through* the priest, and it is from this hierarchical structure that it gets its efficacy. Why? Because it is the image of the whole Mystical Body.

The universal Church is a Body whose head is Christ; in the local church and the liturgical assembly, the head is the priest, as the representative of Christ. But the union of priest and faithful is as close as that of the members of a physical body with its head: it is an organic unity whose parts cannot be isolated. We see then why it is the whole of the local church, the whole assembly that *actively* offers the sacrifice, because all the members are incorporated in its head who is, in the final count, the one true priest: Jesus Christ.

This doctrine of the priesthood of the faithful comes to full flower in that of the already alluded to mystical marriage. The Church, the Universal Church, but equally the local church, is the Bride whose face is turned towards the Lord who presents himself for the wedding: 'and the Spirit and the bride say: Come' (Apoc. 22:17). The Church is the 'spotless Bride of Jesus Christ'.[21] The unanimity of the hearts and voices of the assembly form a single voice, that of the Bride-Church of Christ. Between Groom and Bride a dialogue is established, which is that of the Song of Songs and which resounds in the *Apocalypse* (22:17–20). The efficacy of liturgical prayer is founded upon this nuptial love.

Since, in fact, every dramatic play, and the Mass is one, is made up of an exchange of words and movements, it is important, we think, to

---

21. *Mediator Dei*, 27, after Eph. 5:27.

insist upon this idea of *dialogue*. The Mass presents itself as a double dialogue: dialogue between the priest, the leading actor, and the faithful and dialogue between the congregation and God; the first dialogue is 'horizontal', earthly, the second 'vertical', heavenly, and once again we see the Mass, as dialogue, integrated into the inner cruciform structure we have already studied. The more important dialogue, and ultimately the only one, is the second, the first having as its only purpose to forward, in a manner, the acclamations and prayers from the assembly to the altar, whence they will be raised to heaven.

In order to grasp properly the nature and importance of this dialogue, we need to recall once more that the Mass is accomplished simultaneously on earth and in heaven,

> for there is only one Church in heaven and on earth.... The Divine Liturgy is at the same time accomplished in heaven and on earth ... with this difference, that in heaven it is without veils and symbols, and on earth it is through symbols, for we are encumbered with this burden of a flesh subject to corruption.[22]

There is an extraordinary moment in the Mass. It occurs at the opening of the anaphora, or canon, with the preface and the chanting of the *Sanctus*, the chant of the angels, for then it is as if a door were opened into heaven where we glimpse the mysteries of the Beyond and where we are invited to sing the glory of the Divinity with all the celestial beings. Truly at that moment the liturgy appears as what it really is, an anticipation of heaven, of the celestial life of the elect: 'After knocking down the wall separating heaven and earth,' says St John Chrysostom, 'Christ brought us this canticle of praise from heaven.'[23] 'Join thyself to the holy people, and learn the hidden words,' writes St Gregory of Nyssa, 'proclaim with us what the six-winged cherubim cry out with the Christian people.'[24] The presence of angels during the Mass and our union with the

22. Symeon the New Theologian, PG 155, 337–340.
23. St J. Chrysostom, PG 56, 138.
24. St Gregory of Nyssa, PG 46, 4212c.

angelic choirs have always been strongly emphasized; it is a very old tradition which must go back to the Apostles themselves, for the chanting of the *Sanctus* is found in all liturgies. In those of the East, the presence of the angels is invoked from the start. On entering the sanctuary, the Armenian priest says,

> Lord our God, who established choirs and hosts of angels and archangels for the service of Thy Glory, grant, at this moment when we enter the sanctuary, that Thy holy Angels also enter there as our co-ministers, and together with us glorify Thy Beneficence.

There is an identical prayer in the Byzantine liturgy. The importance of this mentioning of the angels belongs to the fact that the world of the faithful bodiless ones is where God has received a perfect thanksgiving, whereas the same has not happened in the human world, which has not followed the angelic world. But the Redemption has intervened and brought the human world back to the state of the angelic world; the Eucharist restores mankind to the angelic ranks and allows it to participate in the Eucharist of the angels, which is expressed in the *Sanctus*.

The *Sanctus* is made up of two parts: the chant of the Seraphim and the Messianic acclamation. The Seraphic chant is taken from the vision of Isaiah (6:3): '*Sanctus, Sanctus, Sanctus Deus Sabaoth, pleni sunt coeli et terra gloria tua.*' (The text from Isaiah says: 'The earth is full of Thy Glory', that of the Mass, which is more explicit: 'Heaven and earth are full of Thy Glory.')

The acclamation is derived from Psalm 118 (Hallel) and a passage from the Gospel: '*Benedictus qui venit in nomine Domini*' (Psalm 118:26), '*Hosannah in excelsis*' (Matt. 21:9). The passage from St Matthew is that which tells of the triumphal entry of Palm Sunday: 'and the multitudes that went before, and that followed, cried, saying, hosanna to the son of David: blessed is he that cometh in the name of the Lord; Hosanna in the highest.'

This is the royal entry of the messiah, son of David, on earth, sanctioned in a way by the great theophany of the Divine Majesty in heaven in the midst of the Seraphim. Likewise at the Baptism and on Tabor, the earthly scene is sanctioned by the celestial theophany, and at the Nativity, by the chant of the Angels, the *Gloria in excelsis*, which forms part of the Roman Mass.[25]

What is more, the two hymns, the *Gloria* and the *Sanctus* have a similar structure, developing on two registers: *in excelsis* (in heaven) and *in terra* (on earth). In heaven, the splendor of the Divinity (*Gloria in excelsis, Hosanna in excelsis*) and on earth peace to men (*pax hominibus*); because thanks to the coming of the Messenger of God, of Him 'who comes in the Name of the Lord' in the mystery of Christmas, of Palm Sunday, in the glorification of His Passion, commemorated immediately after the *Sanctus* in the Canon, the 'Glory', that is to say the very Radiance of Divinity, descends on earth.

The deep meaning of the *Sanctus*, which is first of all a text from the Old Testament, appears in the *light* of the mystical theology of the Hebrews. According to the latter, God, who is the Infinite, is not manifested directly in the world, which would be impossible, moreover, but, as we have already said,[26] through His Names or Attributes, which the Jews call *Sephiroth*, and which are, in a way, Divine Energies or Powers. Numbering ten, they constitute the Fullness of Being to the extent It is determined and manifested. The three higher *Sephiroth*, Crown, Intelligence, Wisdom, constitute the divine world, the remaining seven correspond to the lower worlds, or, more exactly are the Divine Forces that create and support these worlds. It is quite obvious that this number ten is symbolic, being the number of perfection. Above all it has a qualitative value; it designates the Fullness of Being and, in fact, the indefinite number of the degrees of Universal Existence, of worlds and of beings, the reflection of the Divine Infinity. To the six degrees or *sephiroth* that come after the Divine World correspond the spiritual worlds or angelic states; the tenth *sephira*, called 'Kingdom' (Malkuth) corresponds to the earth and the human world. In the perfect creation, as

25. There is, besides, like a progression from the *Gloria* to the *Sanctus*, a progression that follows that of the Mass itself; the *Gloria* is the chant of the lower angels and this is why, according to St John Chrysostom, it is accessible to the catechumens in the first part of the Mass, whereas the second part introduces us into the mystery of the Trinity and, because of this, is reserved for initiates only, for the baptized.

26. See p90.

it comes forth from the hands of God, the spiritual influx emanating from On-High, from the Crown, descends and circulates normally like blood in the physical organism, crossing all the states, worlds and beings corresponding to the *sephiroth*, down to the tenth, that of our world. This is the state of grace (grace being precisely this spiritual influx) in which God is present in the world. This Divine Presence is the *Shekinah* or Divine Glory. On the other hand, in the state of sin, with the current of grace no longer circulating, the terrestrial world is in a way cut off from God. This is the state of exile, symbolized by the deportation to Babylon, and the loss of the Ark in which the *Shekinah* was manifested before the deportation. It is said then that 'the *Shekinah* is in exile'; this is the great tribulation of Israel and the pious Hebrews pray for the return of the *Shekinah*: 'Lord, fill Thy people again with Thy Glory' (Eccl. 36:16); 'The salvation of God is nigh them that fear Him; that Glory may dwell in our land' (Psalm 84). It is precisely this return of Glory among the people of God, wrought by the Incarnation and Redemption that the *Sanctus* and *Gloria* sing of.

Now the structure of the *Sanctus* is modeled on that of the *Sephiroth*. According to the teaching of the Rabbis, the Sanctus is explained as follows. The three *Sancti* are addressed to the three higher *sephiroth*: Crown, Intelligence, and Wisdom;[27] *Dominus Deus* is addressed to the following three: Love, Rigor, and Beauty: *Sabaoth* to the next three: Victory, Honor, Foundation; and *pleni sunt coeli et terra gloria tua* to the last *sephira*: the Kingdom.[28]

Thus the Seraphic hymn embraces and sums up Creation in its fullness and the Divine Presence within it. It takes us into the mystery of uncreated Being, giving Itself to Itself in the Trinity and causing all being to share in Its own infinite life, a terrible mystery before which the Seraphim themselves cover their faces. But, at the same time, this hymn, like the *Gloria*, proclaims the love of God

---

27. This does not contradict the Trinitarian character of the *Sanctus*, for there is analogy, if not identity, between the three Divine Persons and the three higher *Sephiroth*. It is thus, for example, that the luminous triangle relating to this Ternary is as much a Hebraic as a Trinitarian Christian symbol.

28. Isaac Askenaz in J. Meyer, *De Myster. S. S. Trinitatis.*

that causes His Glory to radiate in everything created and illumi-
nate heaven and earth. It is this love, precisely, that constitutes the
good news of 'Him who comes in the Name of the Lord' in the sacrosanct mystery of the divine liturgy. *Et in terra pax hominibus.* The
peace He brings is not the outer peace, the peace 'as the world gives
it'; it is the 'Peace of the Lord', 'the reconciliation of all things in God
through the blood poured out on the cross' and the fullness of the
state of grace in the soul. The 'Peace of the Lord' is the return from
exile of the '*Shekinah*' who once again 'may dwell in our land',
because 'the Word was made flesh and dwelt among us': *in nobis*,
'among us', but also 'in us' since 'the Kingdom of God is within you'.
And in this way we see all the meaning that this word 'Kingdom'
assumes: *malkuth* is the name of the tenth *sephira*, the dwelling of
God and His Glory among men, His birth among us and in us.[29]

The integration of the *Sanctus* into the eucharistic anaphora
reminds us of the cosmic scope of the sacrifice of the Mass that we
studied above,[30] and allows us to sing and exalt in a truly dignified
(*vere dignum*) way the great mystery of creation and its regeneration
through Christ. The *Sabaoth*, the 'hosts' of the Lord while applying
especially to Victory, Honor and Foundation also designate the stars
(and the angelic choirs that analogously correspond to them)
because the whole hierarchy of these choirs rises up from the earth
to the supreme Being, like the different planetary heavens above us,
beyond the heaven of the fixed stars and, finally, the empyrean
where the eternal fire of the Divinity burns. Thus we have a truly
sacred image of the world, which was that of our ancestors, far
'truer' in reality than that of our modern savants; image of a world
that has itself become chant, a concrete hymn to the Lord: *Cæli
enarrant gloriam Dei.* Man, at the center of the cosmos, is united to
this mute hymn, which is also the hymn of the angels. And since, in
the visible world, it is man alone who has the gift of the word,
speaking and singing, it is for him, on earth, to express through

29. Among the Hebrews, the *Shekinah* is often assimilated to *Malkuth*, the
Kingdom. Moreover, the word *shekinah* comes from a word meaning 'to rest', a
meaning that is similar in many respect to that of 'peace'.

30. See pp19–21, 41–45, and the whole of Chapter 4, p79 ff.

word and song the mute praise of things, to be their spokesman, and celebrate that cosmic liturgy that the angelic choirs celebrate in heaven. That is why, at the end of the Preface, the Church invites us to join our voice with that of the angels to sing the *Sanctus*: 'We *beseech Thee, Lord, grant that we may join with them, ceaselessly repeating: Holy, Holy, Holy, etc.*'

Here, participation in the liturgy is union with the angels who are joined with the assembly of the faithful. According to St John Chrysostom, 'The angels surround the priest. The whole sanctuary and the space around the altar are filled with the heavenly Powers in order to honor Him who is present upon the altar.'[31] In several Eastern liturgies *riphidia* are used; these are circular fans painted or engraved with seraphim, which are carried during the Great Entrance and shaken above the offerings placed on the altar. If the Mass is the representation on earth of the celestial liturgy celebrated by the bodiless hierarchies, we should, in a way, *concelebrate* with them. For we are, 'fellow citizens with the saints, and of the household of God' (Eph. 2:19), and 'are come unto Mount Zion, and unto the city of the living God, the heavenly Jerusalem, and to an innumerable company of angels...' (Heb. 12:22).[32]

The dialogue between the celebrant and the faithful is constantly punctuated with the word *Amen*, which marks their adherence to the prayer or the praise. Its frequency in worship is perhaps why, paradoxically, so little attention is paid to it. Normally, one would ask why it is used so often and why it assumes, so obviously, such importance. *Amen* is a Hebrew word, and if the holy founders of the liturgy, under the inspiration of the Holy Spirit preserved it in its Hebrew form (together with some others like *alleluia, hosanna, sabaoth*), it was clearly for powerful reasons. Its retention in its Hebrew form indicates we are dealing with a particularly sacred

31. *De sacr.* 6, 4.

32. The Byzantine liturgy is even more explicit than the Roman. Introducing the Cherubic Hymn the choir expresses itself thus: 'Let us, who mystically represent the Cherubim and chant the thrice-holy hymn to the Life-giving Trinity. . . .'

word. Hebrew remains, in fact and in principle, the sole sacred language of Christianity, although various circumstances have obliged the use of other languages in both its teaching and liturgy. If, within its sphere, though, Greek, Latin, Syriac, and Arabic are 'liturgical' languages, they are not sacred languages, that is to say immediate depositories of the Divine Word. Directly or indirectly, the whole of Christian teaching and all its formulae have Hebrew as their base and touchstone. And if certain Hebrew words have been kept in the liturgy, this is precisely, in part, to recall this truth. But there are also much more profound reasons. The sacred word *amen* conceals a mysterious teaching, which can only be expressed through the Hebrew form, which also conditions its spiritual efficacy in both public and private prayer.

Amen is connected to the verb *aman*, conveying the idea of 'stability', 'constancy', 'fidelity', and 'truth'. Its root exists in Arabic with a similar meaning. Sometimes it is an adverb, with the meaning of 'yes, in truth' (the word Jesus uses on many occasions: Verily, verily, I say unto you...), and sometimes an adjective and a noun signifying 'true', 'faithful', and 'truth', 'faithfulness', respectively.

It is as an adverb, 'yes, truly', that *amen* serves to conclude prayers; it constitutes the ritual assent of the faithful to the divine praise and to the request addressed to God. This usage is borrowed from Judaism. For example, in Deuteronomy (27:15–26) the people answer *amen* twelve times to the twelve execrations of Moses (upon idolaters, adulterers, etc.). In the Apocalypse, *amen*, sometimes followed immediately by *alleluia*, is the cry of the four Living Beings and the twenty-four elders; they seal the praises of all the creatures of God with an *amen* (Apoc. 5:14, 7:11, 19:4).

Amen is, furthermore, a noun, and, more precisely, a Divine Name, for example in the *Book of Isaiah* (25:1, 65:16), with the meaning of 'God true and faithful', and above all in the Apocalypse, where Christ is called 'Amen, the faithful and true witness, the beginning of the creation of God....' (3:14; cf. 1:5). It is at this last use that we would like to pause, for therein resides the great mystery of *amen*. In fact, over and above its current and outer meaning, the word possesses an inner meaning, which opens perspectives upon the mystery of regeneration.

It is possible to approach the inner meaning thanks to certain methods of interpretation well known to the early Church Fathers and characteristic of sacred languages.

First of all, the word *amen*, in Jewish tradition, is viewed as an abridged Divine Name. That is to say, the three letters AMN (the vowels, in this case the E, not being counted in Semitic languages) constitute an acrostic and are the initials of the three names: *Adonai, Melek, Neeman*, 'Lord', 'King', and 'Faithful'. Applied to Christ, as in the passage from the Apocalypse cited above, this name signifies in the first place faithfulness to the will of the Father, and then the unshakable character of His Royalty, 'whose reign shall have no end' and the certitude that He will fulfill his promises, since He has 'the words of eternal life'.

Secondly, the symbolic value of each letter is considered. 'A' designates the first source, the Principle, the Divine Absolute. 'M' is the sign of Water, the Water of the first chapter of Genesis, that is to say the ensemble of universal possibilities, the 'chaos' that the *Fiat lux* needs to 'organize'. 'N' is the sign of Nature, not so much the nature of modern physicists, but Transcendent Nature (*Natura naturans*) through which the Divine Energy creates the worlds. Thus the word *amen* designates the action of the creative Divine Principle upon universal Nature. Which is exactly the definition of the Divine Word 'through whom all things were made' (John 1:3).

Finally, a gematrical study of the word confirms the preceding sense. In *amen*, by replacing the three consonants with their corresponding numerical values, we get: A (1) + M (40) + N (50) = 91. This sum of 91 can be interpreted in two ways. If one adds the two constituent numbers (an operation called sacred addition), one has: 9 + 1 = 10 = 1 + 0 = 1, which magnificently confirms the meaning obtained by way of the symbolic value of the letters. It means that in the Christ-Amen, and through Him, the whole multiplicity of creatures in nature (M–N) is led back to the Unity of the Father (A), for the Christ-Amen is 'the beginning of the creation of God' (Apoc. 3:14) and 'the first-born of all creatures' (Col. 1:15).

On the other hand, the total 91 is the sum of 26 and 65. Now, 26 corresponds to the numerical value of the Great Name of God (YHWH), and 65 is that of the word *hikal*, 'temple'. From this point of view: Amen = YHWH + hikal, which means this; when *Amen* is realized, the Lord is established in His temple, and, therefore, in the world, of which the temple is the symbol; the divine Presence illumines all beings. Now, it is in the Christ-Amen, yet once again, that the Presence of God in His Creation is realized in a perfect way: the Fullness of God, teaches St Paul, dwelt in Him bodily (Col. 2:9); in His body which is the temple (John 2:21).

These considerations find their whole meaning and justification at a solemn moment in the Mass: the end of the eucharistic prayer. At this point the priest offers to God the whole of creation represented by the bread and wine, the material of the sacrifice, changed into the Body and Blood of Christ, proclaiming,

> Through Whom, Lord, Thou dost ever create, hallow, fill with life, bless and bestow upon us all good things. Through Him, and with Him and in Him, is to Thee, God the Father Almighty, in the union of the Holy Spirit, all honor and glory, world without end.

At this point, the officiant raises the Holy Gifts and the faithful respond: Amen! It is said that in Rome, in the first centuries of Christianity, this *amen* of the people resounded like thunder. This is the great *amen*, the adherence of the people to the sacrifice of expiation and praise; it is like the *amen* chanted by the blessed in the heavenly Jerusalem. On the other hand, as the ritual assembly of believers gathered in the temple for the prayer of sacrifice is, in a certain way, the Mystical Body of Christ, the *Amen*, at this moment, appears as the putting into action of this Divine Name. It is the whole Christ, head and members, who says *Amen* to the glory of God, in conformity with this passage from Scripture: 'For the Son of God, Jesus Christ . . . was not *yea* and *nay*, but in him was *yea* [*amen*]. For all the promises of God in him [Amen = King, Faithful Witness] are *yea*; and in him *Amen* unto the glory of God by us' (2 Cor. 1:19–20).

The Jews say that when one pronounces the word *amen* with all one's might, the doors of heaven open. In fact, at this moment in the Holy Sacrifice, the Victim having been offered, the channel of Grace, broken by the fall is re-established. The state of Eden is restored and

True Man, Celestial Man, the New Adam rises upon the holy stone of the altar, the supreme Mediator between earth and heaven. It is remarkable that as soon as the great *Amen* is pronounced, the Lord's Prayer is chanted. This prayer of the God-Man is, in fact, the summoning of the Reign that the word *amen* symbolizes. When *Amen* = 91 is realized (and it is, virtually, by the Mass), the Will of the Father is done, the Bread of Life abounds, sins are forgiven, there is no more temptation, and evil is driven away, for the Presence of the Lord (YHWH) fills the temple (*hikal*) and the world.

And so, when we say *Amen*, not only at this moment in the sacrifice, but in no matter what prayer, we say our unconditional yes to the Divine Will, in union with the God-Man and proclaim that in Christ the whole of creation returns to God, and that truly heaven is united with earth in the God-Man, in whom we live, being members of His Mystical Body.

6

The Liturgy
of the Word

IN THE COURSE of studying the unfolding of the Mass in an earlier chapter, we mentioned how inadequate the frequently used expressions 'Preface' and 'Preparation' are for describing the first part of the celebration, leaving one to suppose that this phase of the liturgy is not properly speaking the Mass, the latter term only applying to the subsequent phase, that of the sacrifice. Now, nothing could be more erroneous, for the first part of the celebration is an integral part of the Divine Liturgy, forming an inseparable whole with the second. It is a magnificent example of the dialogue between man and God, of which we have spoken, and is made up, in fact, of the prayers of praise and intercession of the faithful addressed to God and His response, which comes to them through the reading of the Bible in the form of the Gospels and the Apostolic Epistles. This reading of the sacred texts, which constitutes the accent and center of this part of the Mass, is the very voice of the Son of God resounding once again in the ears of the Christians. This is why this moment is particularly sacred, and it was a happy initiative, undertaken some years ago, to designate it 'the Liturgy of the Word'. The Mass appears thus to be made up of a double liturgy: the liturgy of the Sacrifice and that of the Word, each answering to and completing the other. The object of the following pages will be to analyze this formula and specify its nature and scope.

Certain people have quite wrongly criticized the expression, claiming that the word 'liturgy' can only be applied to the sacrificial phase, which starts at the offertory. In fact, the formula 'Liturgy of the Word' has a particularly solid foundation, being based in a passage from St Paul, *Romans* 15:16. The Apostle alludes to the grace he has received from God 'to be the minister (*litourgon*) of Jesus Christ to the Gentiles, ministering (*hierourgounta*) the gospel of God, that the offering up (*prosphora*) of the Gentiles might be acceptable, being sanctified by the Holy Spirit.' We have indicated in Greek (and not in the Latin of the Vulgate, which is not exact) the three important words. St Paul is the 'liturgist' of Christ: in the Greek of the New Testament the word *litourgos* always applied to the minister of a cultic function. This is confirmed by the word *hierourgounta,* from the verb *hierourgin,* which designated a cultic act, or the accomplishment of a sacred act (*hieron, ergon*). Finally, the third word, *prosphora,* is the very one designating the offertory and the Holy Gifts in the Mass. Thus the whole passage refers to the context of the Divine Liturgy, the same words serving to designate the oblation and priestly function in the sacrifice being used here to define the ministry of the word, the announcing of the Gospel, which is thus integrated, through the very terminology, into the liturgy of the sacrifice.

This state of affairs is easily explained if we remember that it is one of the oldest, uninterrupted, traditions of the church that the Word of Christ preserved in Scripture is something altogether similar to His Body under the species of bread. St Ignatius of Antioch said that the Gospel was his refuge, 'like the flesh of Jesus';[1] and Origen: 'The bread Christ says is His Body, is the Word that nourishes souls.'[2] Tertullian: 'The Word of life is like the flesh of the Son of God';[3] and St Caesarius of Arles:

> The word of Jesus Christ does not seem to be less estimable than His body. Therefore, just as we take care not to drop the body of Jesus Christ when given to us, even so we should take care not to let the word of Jesus that has been announced to us fall from our hearts. For he is no less culpable who listens to the holy word negligently than he who through his fault lets fall the very body of Jesus Christ.[4]

1. *Ad Phil.* 5, 1.
2. *In Matt. Hom.,* 35.
3. *De resurrect.,* 37.
4. Cited by Bossuet, *Sermon sur la parole de Dieu.*

This is why St Augustine wrote: 'Let us listen to the Gospel as though the Lord Himself were speaking. . . . The Lord dwells On-High, but is likewise here as Truth.'[5] One could follow this tradition of the Church across the ages. Let it suffice to recall that passage from *The Imitation of Christ* which speaks of *two tables* placed in the treasury of the Church: that of the holy altar, where the consecrated bread is found, and that of the Divine Law, containing the holy doctrine that teaches the true faith and leads us even behind the veil where the Holy of Holies is to be found.[6] This is an altogether interesting text, for it lets us understand that a particular divine grace, coming from the mystical union between the proclamation of the Word and the Eucharist, is at work during the course of the Mass. The soul is prepared by the first prayers, such that the Word, when it falls, falls on ground favorable to its germination (Mark 4:8); then comes communion, at which the soul is lifted up by the readings that have revived its faith.

This doctrine of the analogy between Word and Bread explains the marks of veneration surrounding the book of the Gospels. Right from the beginning of the Mass it is placed on the altar to clearly show that it represents Christ. Formerly, at councils and synods, it was placed on a throne to preside over the assembly. In Syrian basilicas the *bema*, the wide estrade in front of the sanctuary intended for the readings, required a small altar upon which the evangelistary was placed. It was surmounted with a canopy on four columns, making it altogether similar to the main altar. This was a practice inherited from the synagogue, where a throne is likewise reserved for the Torah. The solemn procession preceding the reading of the Gospel, with lights, the censing of the book, and its kissing, which recalls the kissing of the altar—which 'is' Christ—all these rites tend in the same direction of a veritable liturgy and adoration addressed to the Word of God.[7]

But why, it will be asked, this need to read the Gospel, as well as

---

5. *Treatise* 30 *In Joh.*, 1 (P.L. 35, 1632).

6. *The Imitation of Christ*, 4, chap. 11.

7. In the East, during the course of the Mass, the priest blesses the assembly with the evangelistary just as with the cross.

the Epistles, which are but commentaries on it? Is it not sufficient that each of the faithful read the Holy Scriptures in private? No, because, for intrinsic reasons, the Holy Scriptures ought to be communicated during divine worship. First, because that is what they were composed for, to be the catechism addressed to the *ecclesia*, the assembly, the *synaxis*, gathered for the liturgy. Then, as recalled above, because the Church believes Christ to be alive in the word of the Apostle and the Evangelists, and that the Christ speaking through these texts is a Christ *present* in the assembly. Christ Himself guarantees His presence to the faithful gathered together in His Name: 'For where two or three are gathered together in my name, there am I in the midst of them.'[8] Thus, the synaxis is the place and privileged moment for the communication of the Word of God. God is active in the 'proclamation' (*kerygma*) of His Word, to which the faithful adhere through their 'acclamation': *Laus tibi, Christe, Doxa si, Christe.*

It is necessary in such cases to be thoroughly aware of the reality before which we find ourselves, and how it is produced. The words *revealed* in the Scriptures are *actualized* through ritual recitation. Among the rabbis, liturgical reading is comparable to the direct emission of the Divine Voice at Sinai. This moreover is why the liturgical reading should be done according to a certain rhythm, about which we shall have more to say, and, if it is not psalmodized, should be done *recto tono*. There is no greater mistake than to want to make of the Gospel or the epistle an 'expressive' reading, according to the rules of profane diction. For then a man necessarily puts something of himself into it; whereas, in this instance, the personality of the human individual should be effaced before the transcendent personality of the Divine Master. The solemn and ritual reading of the Word of the Master realizes the immediate presence of the original act through which it was manifested the first time, *in*

---

8. Matt. 18:20. This affirmation is taken from the Jewish tradition. In fact, we read in *Pirke Aboth* 3, 8; 'Whence cometh it that, when ten men are assembled for prayer, the *Shekinah* is in the midst of them? ... And whence cometh it that, when two are assembled to study the Law, the *Shekinah* is in the midst of them?' We have already had occasion, it seems, to evoke the correspondences of Christ with the *Shekinah*, which is the 'dwelling of God among men'. See p 81, n 4.

illo tempore. The words pronounced cause the original act to arise anew, and the reality of salvation of which they are bearers, becomes present among us.[9] This is realized according to the mode we have already described for the sacrifice: in the same manner as for the consecration of the Bread and the Wine, it is the power of the Holy Spirit, descending through the intermediary of the Church, that vivifies the action of the Church, the action of the celebrant. Thus this solemn reading of the Scripture is truly a *sacrament of the Word*, and one understands better now the close connection between Word and Sacrifice in the Mass. The word that speaks in the liturgy is that Word through which the world was created, the Logos, and through which the world needs to be recreated, which is the very purpose of the Holy Sacrifice as restoration of the original world. In this word, its Author is effectively present. This is why one should not regard the scripture passages proclaimed in the Mass as articles of dogma, as expressions of ideas or concepts after the manner of scholarly texts. No, they constitute, as has been said, a 'call'. The people of God are called by the Word to do and become that which the Word proclaims. The people respond to that call through an engagement; the liturgical celebration engages the people insofar as the Mass, as we have said, is the cult of the mystical Body. Accordingly, the proclamation of Scripture at the Mass is something quite different from some reading or other, however interesting it might be. The whole Mass is ultimately a 'Liturgy of the Word'; the liturgy of the one and only Word who spoke at the beginning of the world, who, 'at the end of the ages', has spoken as the Word made Flesh (*Verbum caro factum est*), and who, at this moment, during the Divine Liturgy, *speaks* anew to man and is given to him as *food* so as to be able, from man's very heart, to sing the praise of the Father in the Holy Spirit.

An important point, to which we return in order to insist upon it, is that the sacred texts preserving the word of God should be communicated *orally* by the priest to the faithful. Once again, we

---

9. This fact is a constant in all religious areas; thus the ritual reading—which is a celebration—of the cosmogonic account constitutes a reiteration of the creation; for example at the Babylonian New Year festival (see M. Eliade, *The Myth of the Eternal Return*, 1954, pp73–74, and *Myth and Reality*, 1963, *passim*).

are faced here with a constant of the universally sacred, especially of the cults we have studied in connection with sacrifice and ritual commemoration, which, following the Greeks, are called 'mysteries', and which exist in the majority of traditions, and to the form of which the Christian cult is connected. We have seen that one characteristic of these cults is to enable the believer, the 'myst', to share in the destiny of the god through the intermediary of rites, which are arranged in three categories: liturgical *actions* (*dromena*), *showings* (*deiknymena*) of sacred objects, and *sayings* (*legomena*). This last type of rite consists in revealing to the believer the story of the god, which is the story of salvation. Here we have exactly what we are calling the 'liturgy of the word'. Now, in all the cults, the transmission of the story of the god is the *oral* transmission of a secret, the secret of salvation (*sotira*) and that transmission is made from mouth to ear; the priest 'transmits' (*paradidosi*) and the faithful 'receives' (*paralamvani*). St Paul expresses himself nowise differently when he writes: 'For this cause also thank we God without ceasing, because when ye received (*paralavontes*) the word of God which ye *heard* of us (*logon akois*), ye received it not as the word of men, but as it is in truth the word of God, which effectually worketh also in you that believe' (1 Thess. 2:13). The mystagogue 'speaks' and the disciple 'hears' and 'receives'. He receives the divine word, not through writing, but from the living voice, in a living process, a living contact, and from the mouth of someone who has himself received it through a transmission (*paradosis*), or if one prefers, a tradition, uninterrupted since the founder of the cult, in the case of Christianity, through the 'apostolic chain'.

St Paul insists on the necessity of oral transmission for the evangelical message: 'So then faith cometh by hearing,' he says, and adds, 'and hearing through the word of Christ' (*pistis ex akois, hi de akoi dia rimatos Christou*) (Rom. 10:17). 'Faith cometh by hearing', the hearing of the voice of the Apostle and the voice of the Church, for the voice of the Church is the emanation of the Divine Word.

The soundness of this oral communication of the Word of God has been made especially clear by the researches of Fr. P. Jousse on the anthropology of word and gesture, which have opened a new way into the understanding of Scripture.

This scholar has recalled that the *word* designating a thing can be the thing just as well as the thing itself, because the word itself is fundamentally concrete. This is especially true of the languages of traditional societies like that of the ancient Hebrews, where the *word* and the *name* (Hebrew *shem*) are synonyms for *essence*, for the *nature* of a being or an object. The word is fundamentally an articulation projected outwards by the breath and received by the ear. The organ of articulation is the mouth of him who speaks; now the mouth, the organ of speech, is also the instrument of eating. Regarding this, Fr Jousse has been able to point out a passage from Plato which already conspicuously indicated the ambivalent role of the mouth:

[Our] framers [the gods] ... framed the mouth, as now arranged, having teeth and tongue and lips, with a view to the necessary and the good, contriving the way in for necessary purposes, the way out for the best purposes. For that is necessary which enters in and gives food to the body, but the river of speech, which flows out of a man and ministers to the intelligence, is the fairest and noblest of all streams.[10]

The word, Fr Jousse continues, is incorporated (and this word should be given the full force of its etymology, for it means, 'to cause to enter or penetrate the body') by the bone and tympanum of the one who hears. But, in addition, it is incorporated equally by his mouth, because man is, by nature, a mimic, who repeats, in micro-movements, the visible cheek movements of the speaker. Thus the word, a meaningful vibration, is cast from the body of the speaker to become a part of the body of the listener, and this by way of hearing and mimicking. It is upon this psychosomatic process that teaching in traditional societies is based, in particular in the Palestinian milieu, which was that of Christ. Mouthing, as Fr Jousse says, is the human movement chosen by God for His teaching. Now, to mouth is at the same time to speak, to recite, and to eat, as we have already said. Moreover, in this same Palestinian milieu, the teacher gave his lessons in a rhythmo-melody, which facilitated

10. *Timaeus,* 75D,E [Jowett trans.].

penetration among the taught, and with movements, an appropriate miming, such that the teaching was also received through the eyes. Through exposure to this melody and mime, the master was literally *incarnated* in the disciple. The teaching penetrated deeply into his psychosomatic being through an intussusception (from Latin *suscipere* 'to receive', 'to take', *intus*, 'to the interior', 'into the innermost'). In this type of teaching, the disciple replays the lesson of the master; it is 'repeated in *echo*' (in Greek *catecho*, whence the word *catechism*). This is what the Jews call the *mishna*. One learnt the Torah in this way by 'repeating in echo' the Word of God, and such was the practice in the liturgy of the synagogue; it is the normal function of distributing the word, the synagogue being considered a replica of Sinai. And this is equally the fundamental conception of the Christian cult.

What is most characteristic in this intussusception of the word is what Fr Jousse calls the *eating of the word*; one takes the words of the master into one's mouth and eats them. Thus God, speaking to Ezekiel, said to him,

> 'Open thy mouth, and eat that I give thee.' And when I looked, behold an hand was sent unto me; and, lo, a roll of a book was therein.... And he said unto me, 'Son of man, eat that thou findest; eat this roll, and go speak unto the house of Israel.' So I opened my mouth and he caused me to eat that roll.... 'Son of man, cause thy belly to eat, and fill thy bowels with this roll that I give thee.' Then did I eat it; and it was in my mouth as honey for sweetness' (Ezek. 2:10; 3:1–3).[11]

One finds, moreover, a similar sequence in the *Apocalypse* (10:8–9).

To the extent possible, every teacher, says Fr Jousse, gives himself to be eaten; true pedagogy consists in incarnating the whole being of the master in the disciple. Jesus, who is the Almighty, realized this in a perfect way at the Last Supper. As Fr Jousse puts it:

---

11. Cf. Psalm 118:129–131, 'Thy testimonies are wonderful: therefore doth my soul keep them.... I opened my mouth, and panted: For I longed for thy commandments.' Cf. the popular expression 'to drink in somebody's words'.

The Last Supper is indissolubly the buccal and oral intussusception of the flesh and blood of the Teacher and the buccal and oral
intussusception of His rhythmo-catechism; these are the Last
Supper and the Discourse after the Last Supper [of St John].[12]

Fr Jousse's sentence, coming after the summary of his anthropology
we have just made, clearly shows how the Church, following in the
footsteps of Christ and the Apostles, conceives the heart of its teaching, the solemn proclamation of Scripture, of the Word of God. Let
us note, moreover, that a rhythmo-melody contributes to this
solemnity, which, as we have said, also has as its goal to facilitate the
innermost penetration, the incarnation, the intussusception of the
Word in the psychosomatic being of the believer. This rhythmo-
melody is inherited from the Jewish practice; reduced to a very simple line in the Latin rite, it has kept all its richness and efficacy in the
Eastern rites. One needs to hear, for example, the solemn proclamation of Scripture in Arabic or Rachmaninov's extraordinary
rhythmo-melodic arrangement of the *Epistle to the Romans*, in the
Slavo-Byzantine rite, to understand the gulf that separates such
proclamations from the pitiful, so-called 'expressive' reading that
has become general in the western Church. Here, it is a small
human breath, without much reach, that hardly fits the sublimity of
the message; there, on the contrary, it is truly an echo of the Great
Voice that resounded at Sinai, or upon the Mount of the Beatitudes,
a proclamation worthy of the Divine Word.

Fr Jousse's studies clearly reveal the connection between annunciation of the word of God and eucharist, between eucharistic liturgy, subsequently, and liturgy of the word. In both cases, it is a
question of our incorporating, under two different modes, 'the flesh
and blood', that is to say, according to the Biblical expression, the
whole being of the Son of God, of the Divine Word.

Thus, if this conception conditions the mode of announcing the
Word of God in the liturgy, it at the same time dictates our attitude
vis-à-vis this Word and the way in which it should be received. The

---

12. We are summarizing here the essential of two works of Fr Jousse: *L'anthropologie du geste*, Paris, 1969, and *La manducation de la parole*, Paris, 1975.

Word should to be *eaten* because it needs to become flesh of our flesh and spirit of our spirit. We need to let ourselves be invested with it and the force of the Spirit, and it should form a substantial word in the heart, through a sort of infusion in a way similar to that of the infusion of consciousness into the body. And it is to this that the three signs of the cross refer that one traces before the hearing of the Gospel on one's forehead, mouth and chest; these three places of the body correspond in fact to three centers of the subtle organism that condition spiritual 'awakening'.[13] According to a symbolism familiar to scripture, one could also say that the Word of God should fall, like the grain of wheat, into the 'earth' of our bodies and our hearts so as to germinate there (Matt. 13:4–23). This is a very far-reaching symbolism, for it leads us to the threshold of the mystery of the Incarnation; in the text of the Maronite Mass, we read these words placed in the mouth of Christ Himself:

> Our Lord said: I am the Bread of Life descended from heaven upon earth in order that the world live through Me. The Father sent Me, the Bodiless Word: like a delightful grain of wheat in a fertile earth, the womb of Mary received Me. . . .

The Logos, or Word, should be born in us as in the womb of the Virgin. But how is it born there? Through hearing. This is the mystery of the Annunciation, the Great Announcing of the Word, of the Logos. Now, according to St Augustine, the Virgin conceived in the first place through hearing, by listening to the Word, and it was through obedience to the Divine Word that she was worthy to conceive in her body;[14] *fiat mihi secundum verbum tuum, et Verbum caro factum est.* Mary's *fiat*, the same word that caused the creation to arise—*fiat lux, et lux facta est*—caused the Divine Word, the Divine Logos, to be conceived in a human body. The Annunciation is thus the archetype of listening to the Word of God. To illustrate this mystery of the Annunciation and also, consequently, of listening to the

---

13. In terms of the Hindu terminology—which is serviceable—we are dealing here with the three *chakras* called *ajna* (at the forehead), *vishudda* (at the throat), and *anahata* (at the heart).

14. Cited by Bossuet, *Sermon sur la parole de Dieu.*

Word, we shall cite a page written by the Sufi Al-Baqli, which well describes the process of this spiritual generation:

> The substance of Mary is the very substance of original Sanctity. Reared by the Real [the Divinity], in the light of Intimacy, she was, each time she breathed, magnetized by the signs of Proximity and Intimacy, towards the hearth of Divine Lights; at every moment, she was on the look out for the rising of the Sun of Power to the East of the Kingdom. Through her lofty aspiration, penetrated with the light of the hidden Mystery, she withdrew far from all created beings. She turned towards the horizon whence the glimmerings of the Essence and the Attributes of God flash, inhaling the breezes of union which blow from the world of Eternity. Towards her came one of the breezes of the eternal Meeting, and over her the sun of the contemplation of Sanctity rose. When she contemplated the manifestation of the East bursting with the Eternal, Its lights would invade her and Its secrets reach right to the depths of her soul. Her soul *conceived through the Breath of the Hidden Mystery. She became the bearer of the most-high Word* [the Divine Logos] and of the Light of the most exalted Spirit. When her state became magnified through the reflection in her of the beauty manifesting the Eternal, she hid herself far from creatures, placing her joy in the espousals of the [supreme] Reality.[15]

---

15. Cited by Fr Abd-al-Jalil, *Marie et l'Islam*, Paris, 1950.

7

Theosis

HAVING in the last chapters studied several modalities of the Divine Liturgy, we need now, at the end of this work, to return to its central object, to analyze it yet further and assess its ultimate reach.

The central object of the liturgy, we have said, is the Mystery of Christ; and the Mystery of Christ is consumed in the reality of the sacrifice understood in its widest sense.

We are not going to repeat all we have already said on these two realities. It is enough to recall that the Mystery of Christ is the whole economy of His incarnation, death, resurrection, ascension, and the outpouring of the Holy Spirit; that the sacrifice of Christ is also everything that is actualized for man in the rite of the Divine Liturgy. And, precisely, we would like now to resume examining these two realities, by considering them more especially in their ground and their ultimate end, namely the sanctifying transformation of man.

Concerning the nature and scope of this transformation, there can be no doubt: it is a question of deification, or *theosis*. This is clearly evident from the great discourse pronounced by Christ Himself after the Last Supper:

> That they all may be one, as thou, Father, art in me and I in thee, that they also may be one in us: that the world may believe that thou hast sent me. And the glory which thou gavest me I have given them; that they may be one, even as we are one: I in them and thou in me, that they may be made perfect in one.... (John 17:21–23).

And in another passage, Jesus beseeches the Father that, 'there where I am, they may be also.'

Here we have the fundamental charter of *theosis*, if we may so express it. St Paul will repeat the same thing in different words: 'God . . . has quickened us together with Christ, and hath raised us up together, and made us to sit together in heavenly places in Jesus Christ' (Eph. 2:4–6). As a vesperal hymn for the feast of the Ascension in the Byzantine rite comments: 'This nature, O God, the nature of Adam that fell into the depths of the earth, and that You renewed, You raise today together with Yourself above the Principalities and Powers. In Your love for it, You establish it even there where You live.' Likewise St Leo: 'We have not only been affirmed today as possessors of paradise, but in the person of Christ, have penetrated to the highest of the heavens. . . . The Son of God, has incorporated mankind and placed it at the right hand of the Father.'[1] In a different form, St Paul again announces the same transformation when he says: 'Christ is the image of God' and 'we are changed into the same image from glory to glory, even as by the Spirit of the Lord' (2 Cor. 4:4 and 3:18).

What Scripture expresses in existential and imaginative terms, the Fathers and the Tradition after it translate into metaphysical terms, in which the depth of the mystery can be seen very clearly. St Gregory of Nyssa writes:

> Having finished the creation of man, who was completely new and altogether beautiful, God said to him: 'O Man, you will be the master of the earth and superior to all that exists in the universe. You will be equal to Me, your God. As pledge of your resemblance to God, I give you, at once, the divine prerogative par excellence: freedom.[2]

Was this not, moreover, but a first degree, so to say, as the expression 'at once' suggests, supposing as it does that something else is to follow. Man was called to a higher realization than 'equality', to which allusion is made. Likewise, in another passage, the same Father writes this lapidary formula, flashing like a thunderbolt:

---

1. Lesson of the second nocturne of the Ascension, in the Latin rite.
2. St Gregory of Nyssa, PG 46, 524A.

'Man was conceived with the command to become God.'[3] A formula that is not isolated, being found among other Fathers: 'God mixed His blood with ours to make us, mankind, a single being with Him';[4] 'Christ was incarnated so that man might become God,'[5] a formula that summarizes the theanthropic 'journey'.

In its ultimate depths, then, the mystery of Christ, about which we have been speaking since the beginning of this book, is deification. And this deification is realized in the Mass, as Christ Himself let it be understood by pronouncing the words cited above just after the Last Supper, in which He instituted the eucharistic sacrament. St Maximus the Confessor said it in striking terms: 'Through holy participation in the pure and life-giving mysteries [the Mass], man receives intimacy and *identity with God: in this way it is given to man to become God, from man that he was.*'[6] The liturgy itself recalls it, whence this Secret prayer from the Latin rite: 'O God, Who dost make us partakers of Thy Supreme Godhead by means of the communion in this adorable Sacrifice, grant, we pray Thee, that since we know Thy truth, we may live up to it by a worthy life. Through Our Lord. . . .'[7]

And above all, still in the Latin rite, the prayer we have already commented upon, accompanying the mixing of the water and wine at the offertory.

O God, who hast established the nature of man in wondrous dignity and even more wondrously hast renewed it, grant that through the mystery of this water and wine, we may be made partakers of His divinity, who has deigned to become partaker of our humanity, Jesus Christ.

---

3. Ibid., PG 36, 560A.

4. St John Chrysostom, *Hom.* 46, 2 (PG 49, 260).

5. St Augustine, cf. St Irenaeus, *Adv. Haeres.* 5 (PG 7, 1 120); St Athanasius, *De incarn. verbi* 54 (PG 25, 192B); St Gregory Nazianzus, *Poem. dogm.*, 10, 5 –9 (PG 37, 465); and once again, St Gregory of Nyssa, *Orat. catech.*, 25 (PG 45, 65D). For a continuation, see Eckhart: 'The soul is united to God like food to man, becoming the eye within the eye, the ear within the ear; thus in God the soul becomes God, for I am what absorbs me rather than myself' (Evans I, 287 and 380).

6. St Maximus the Confessor, *Mystag.* 24 (PG 91, 704).

7. Secret for the 18th Sunday after Pentecost

We shall, moreover, in a moment have to return once more to this rite of the mixing.

All the texts just cited clearly say that the Mass is the place where deification is realized by means of a veritable transmutation of man. The process of the Divine Liturgy is therefore not dissimilar to that of alchemy. In fact, in both cases there is a simultaneous transformation, or transmutation, of both a material element and the man engaged in the operation.

No one should be surprised that we mention alchemy here. We know that generally among the public, especially Catholics, alchemy has a bad image, being ranked among the accursed, more or less satanic, sciences, though quite wrongfully so. Doubtless there have been dubious, even sometimes satanic alchemists, like the legendary Dr Faust. But this should not cause one to ignore the genuine and good alchemy of the true alchemists, who include in their ranks men famous in religion and for their sanctity, such as Basil Valentine, Gerbert, who became pope, the Franciscans Roger Bacon and Raymond Lull, and St Albert the Great, the master of St Thomas Aquinas, who, if he himself did not practice alchemy, nevertheless valued this science as he did also true astrology. It is regrettable that Catholic authors who write about these traditional sciences are, for the most part, ignorant of their true nature, knowing only their more or less occult deviations.

Alchemy, in the strictest sense, aimed at realizing the 'Philosopher's Stone', which is able to transmute diverse metals into gold. In general, of the whole of alchemy, only this last trait has been retained, which is not its most important. The most important was not so much the transmutation of ordinary metals into gold, but the obtainment of the Philosopher's Stone through the transmutation of a preliminary material. This 'primary matter' of the alchemical work was a mixture of three substances: Sulphur, Mercury, and Salt, which, to tell the truth, were considered less in terms of their physical nature than as supports of three cosmological principles. The 'Great Work' consisted in transforming the mixture of these three substances, which was placed in the 'Philosopher's Egg', and submitted to the fire of the athanor. The process required three phases called, in their order of appearance, the black, the white, and the red work. The material obtained at the end of the process was the famous 'Philosopher's Stone', a sublimated material—the receptacle of universal energy, the *spiritus mundi*—capable of transforming metals into gold.

Such was operative alchemy, the work of which was accomplished in the laboratory. Among the true alchemists, however, this work was only the outer aspect of alchemy. Operative alchemy was only the outer aspect of what was called spiritual alchemy, the goal of which was the transformation of man, his spiritualization. In sum, one has here, in the case of a particular occupation, the same double structure as in other occupations in traditional societies; those of architect, for example, or potter, etc. For in such societies, occupations are considered as supports, each adapted to a particular vocation, for the spiritualization of those involved in them. The different elements and tools of the occupation become symbols of spiritual realities and, as such, enter into the *rites* of the occupation because, in an occupation conceived in this way, all operations are *rites*.[8] Thus, in alchemy, the primary matter represented coarse man, ordinary man, while the Philosopher's Stone stood for spiritualized man, at the end of the three stages of progression represented by black, white and red. One finds this symbolism, to cite but one case, with the German mystic Angelus Silesius, who used these material operations of alchemy to designate the phases of the mystical apprehension of the Divinity.

If the similarity between the Mass and alchemy is obvious when considered in their general design, is it possible also to discover analogies in the details? Attempts have been made to compare the three phases of the Great Work with certain sequences of the liturgy; but the results obtained are not at all convincing and for the most part arise from arbitrary and forced comparisons. In reality, what can be compared to the three phases of the Great Work are the degrees of Christian initiation: baptism, confirmation, and eucharist. Baptism, in fact, corresponds completely to the black work, which, like it, is a symbolic 'death'. Confirmation, the complement

---

8. One can see a first approach to this problem in our book *Divine Craftsmanship: Preliminaries to a Spirituality of Work*.

of baptism, is, like the white work, a 'resurrection' in a new form through the power of the Spirit. The eucharist, finally, the sacrament of union, is, like the red work, the final accomplishment of the transformation, such that the Mass, in its general design, corresponds quite well to the red work, and there is no need in our view to search, in the global structure, for correspondences, *at the same level*, with the first two phases of the alchemical process. Having said this, one should not be prevented from discovering certain analogies between several elements of the eucharistic celebration and those of alchemy. Among Christian alchemists, Christ, already assimilated to the stone of Jacob, as we have shown in connection with the altar, has quite correctly been compared to the Philosopher's Stone, the symbolic expression of transcendent man. Another definite analogy is that between the cup of the sacrifice, the chalice, and the 'Philosopher's Egg', also called the 'hermetic vessel': both are the receptacle of a 'primary matter'. In the preparatory phase of the eucharistic sacrifice, the priest mixes wine and water in the chalice, and we have seen in an earlier chapter, and also a moment ago, the capital importance of this rite for understanding the meaning of the Mass. The wine, here, is already the blood, as one is led to understand by the prayer accompanying the rite in the Eastern liturgies and referring to the stroke of the centurion's spear and to the blood mixed with water that issued from the side of the crucified one. Now, in St John we read this affirmation: 'And there are three that bear witness on earth, the Spirit, and the water, and the blood' (1 John 5:8). The water and the blood are in the chalice and, immediately after mixing them, the priest, in the Latin rite, calls upon the Spirit, to descend upon the Gifts. Now it has been remarked that the ternary Blood-Water-Spirit reminds one of the alchemical ternary, Sulphur-Mercury-Salt, which, as we have seen, constitutes the mixture placed in the Philosopher's Egg. In spiritual alchemy, the animic mercury becomes a burning 'water' under the influence of the sulphur, which corresponds to the blood, that is to say the wine transformed by the salt, which is the Spirit. These analogies become more precise and clearer when we remember that, in spiritual alchemy, the three substances are symbols of the process of man's metaporphosis. We see then that, in both cases, the 'material' prepared before the Great Work and before the consecration, represents the ordinary common individual man, who will be transmuted and become spiritual man and, in the Eucharist, the archetypal God-Man of the whole of renewed creation. Or, to use St Paul's words, the 'old man' disappears to make way for the 'new man', whose archetype is Christ. From this point of view, then, one perceives something in the Divine Liturgy that corresponds to the 'black work'. The faithful, in participating in the eucharistic mystery, 'die' with Christ, that is to say put the 'old man' to death, for, as St Paul says: 'know that our old man is crucified with him (Christ) (Rom. 6:6). This death is that which precedes the resurrection—the 'white work'—except that the 'black work' and 'white work' are concomitant in the consecration, for it is a question here of theurgy, of action operated directly by God so that there is neither before nor after. Christ present in the Gifts is, in one and the same moment, Christ dead and Christ resurrected; and the same goes for the faithful who in communion share in His mystery, which can then be considered, *from the point of view of the faithful*, as the 'red work'.

If we have spent some time on the correspondences between the Mass and alchemy, this is because their examination, by throwing new light on the notion of sacrifice, enables us to better sketch, it seems to us, the profile of the operation realized in the Divine Liturgy. With this examination we need to remember that the operation develops on two planes; that of its *objective* reality and that of the *subjective* reality of the man engaged in it. The objective reality is that of the Gifts changed into the very person of Christ; and the subjective reality is that of the faithful transformed through participation in the consecrated Gifts and, thereby, incorporated in the Person of Christ.

From this angle, but better clarified, it seems to us, we meet again the mechanism of sacrifice. To recall it, let us take the very suggestive definition the Hindu tradition gives it: 'The sacrificant[9] passes from the state of men to that of gods.' How? 'The sacrifice is the

---

9. The sacrificant is he who offers the sacrifice, the believer. The sacrificer is the priest. But it goes without saying that what is said of the sacrificant is equally valid for the sacrificer, in as much as the latter *also* acts as a sacrificant.

other Self of the gods. . . . This is why the sacrificant, having made the sacrifice, his other Self takes his place in heaven, that world of the gods.'[10] This can be translated into a series of three 'equations' that are articulated in the following syllogism: The sacrifice, the offering, 'is' the god; now, the sacrificant is identified with the sacrifice; therefore the sacrificant is identified with the god. The effect, so to say, of this mechanism is, as was shown in the first chapter, that the gift has an ambivalent nature: it is, simultaneously, the believer and the god. It is the believer to the extent it is given by him; it is the god to the extent that, being offered, it passes from man to god. In alchemical language, there is therefore a double transmutation: that of the material of the sacrifice and that of the sacrificant into one and the same divine entity. In the case of the Divine Liturgy this mechanism of the sacrifice is admirably shown: it follows from the text, already cited on several occasions, that accompanies the mixing of wine and water, and from many passages of the liturgy. It was very clearly revealed in the ancient rite of the offertory, unfortunately abandoned for a long time now, in which the faithful in procession brought the material of the sacrifice to the altar. It is not important, for the reality remains the same. Man brings his gift, which represents him. God takes it and changes it into His own Being and, in communion, gives it back to man so that he might be transformed, in his turn, and penetrate into the Divine Being. At final count, the whole eucharistic liturgy leads back to this very simple but absolutely transcendent pattern, which perfectly expresses the sacramental realization of the theanthropic mystery.

Ultimately, the sacrifice is the sacrifice of man, the sacrifice man makes of himself, as was shown at the beginning of the book. The gift, a thing or living being that constitutes the sacrificial material, is a substitute for the sacrificant. The gift is a part of the personality, a part which, through a sort of existential metonymy stands for the whole, and which acts as such in the operation of the sacrifice. Fundamentally, then, the sacrifice is the sacrifice of the person; sacrifice, to be understood in its already noted ambivalence as immolation

10. *Satapatha Brahmana*, VIII, 6, 1, 10.

and sacralization. In the act of sacrifice, the personality of the sacrificant simultaneously undergoes immolation and sanctification, in this sense that it is withdrawn from the profane world to be transferred to the divine world. Thus we find again the notions developed in the first chapter and the alchemical process explained a moment ago.

But in what do both immolation and transfer to the divine world consist? In this, that, fundamentally, *the sacrifice is the sacrifice of the ego and the emergence of the Self.* The personality of man, in fact, is formed of the ego and the Self. The ego is the empirical individuality, the exterior of the man; it is a limited thing that the Self surpasses infinitely. In order to avoid in advance all misunderstanding, let us immediately say that we do not intend by the Self the meaning given to it by modern psychology, in particular the school of Freud or even Jung. For these the notion is very restricted, whatever may be said of it, from the fact that they only envisage the study of man from the psychological point of view. As for us, we employ the word Self in the traditional sense, that is to say that we see there a reality of a far superior order, that of ontology and even metaphysics. The Self is the very foundation of the person in the strict sense; it is the transcendent personality, totally spiritual, whose center is what the mystics call the 'interior castle' and Eckhart, the 'Ground', *Grund.* It is a hypercosmic reality, it is 'god in man' and, to use the terms of *Genesis,* the 'image of God in man'. In sacrifice, the immolation falls upon the ego. The limiting elements of the personality, the source of separation, conflicts, sin and to say it all, egoism, are immolated with the entire ego, as the concretion of egoism, and at the same stroke, the Self, a prisoner in a way of the ego, is liberated. From that moment, man is established in his proper center and basic identity as 'son of God'. It is this that Christ, the God-Man, accomplished in His sacrifice, once and for all, for man; this is why He is the archetype of the total sacrifice through which the sacrifice of other men can be effected. Christ, says St Paul, 'crucified the old man,' that is to say the ego, and was thus raised as the 'new man', in the *corpus glorificationis,* that is to say the Self, and became Him who, dare we say, brings forth from the Self every man that is incorporated in Him.

It is this that is actualized in the Divine Liturgy, on the two planes, the objective and subjective, that we have mentioned. The Gifts, which are man's offering, are immolated virtually at the offertory, and effectively at the consecration. They lose all their materiality, which is symbolically expressed in the elevation of the offering towards heaven, the spiritual world; they are 'sublimated' and become a *corpus volatile*, as the alchemist would say, and finally, are completely transubstantiated into the Body and Blood of Christ, becoming a *corpus glorificationis*. All of which takes place on the objective plane. But, as the Gifts 'are' also the sacrificant, on the subjective plane the sacrificant, through their mediation, is immolated as to his ego,[11] also sublimated, and finally seized by the divine power and incorporated in the Lord in whom his Self comes to full bloom. The man who 'through Christ, with Christ and in Christ' (*per ipsum, et cum ipso et in ipso*) has thus abandoned his ego, and in whom the Self has emerged, is, by that very fact, established in his own center, whence he perceives everything, both in and around himself, with the very eye of God. This is the personal realization of theanthropy which caused St Paul to say: 'It is no longer I who live, but Christ who lives in me.'

The place and the instrument of this transubstantiation of man, which is the consequence and fruit of the transubstantiation effected at the altar, is the cross, where with Christ we put the 'old man' to death in order to resuscitate the 'new man'. The structure of the cross, studied above with regard to the structure of the celebration, is the symbolical expression of this transubstantiation. On the universal plane, its two axes symbolize the whole extent of the created, as has been said, and on the individual plane, all the constituent elements of the personality, its egoic tendencies—the horizontal axis—and its spiritual propensities—the vertical axis. At the intersection of the two axes, the ego comes to die, or, if one prefers, to be sublimated, keeping only those elements conducive to ascension; the point of intersection of the two axes is the 'place' of the Self, the

---

11. In the Byzantine Mass, at the moment of the offertory, the congregation pronounces these words: 'We offer ourselves, and each other and our whole life unto Christ our God.' Cf. St Paul, Rom. 12:1 and St Augustine, *Civ. Dei*, 10, 20.

central point. In iconography, it is sometimes ornamented with the radiating Heart or the Rose, two symbols of the blossoming of the Self and of *theosis*.

When man has thus integrated his divine personality, one can say that the 'image of God' in him has rejoined its heavenly archetype, which is the metaphysical definition of salvation. It is, at the same time, the act whereby the 'sacrifice of God', about which we have spoken and which is like the exteriorization of God in His creation, is, dare we say, annulled, or 'redeemed'. For, in this act, man renounces his exteriorized state so as to remake, in an inverse sense, the journey of God towards the creature, in such a way that the creature returns to its Principle. And, with it, the whole of creation, because man, in integrating the Self, does not take the road of return to God alone. As microcosm, the mirror and summary of the world, he leads the whole cosmos along this road, in the footsteps of Christ, who, as God-Man—God, certainly, but also man—first wrought the redemption of the whole cosmos.

This spiritual alchemy is represented symbolically in Andrew Rublev's wonderful and much celebrated icon of the Trinity.[12] In order to summarize the meaning and importance of the eucharistic sacrifice in its relationship to the whole economy of salvation, we can do no better, at the end of this work, than to relate the teaching, both hidden and open, of this icon.[13]

The work is intended to be a representation of both the Divine Essence and the work of salvation, or the realization of the King-dom, which is the immaterial and unconditioned presence of the Divinity. The gazes of the 'angels', turned one towards the other, express the enstasis of the Divine Essence. The movement which starts from the foot of the angel on the right—the Holy Spirit—continues in the inclination of his head, passes through the central angel—the Son—takes in the Cosmos, figured by the tree and the

12. The icon is also called the 'Theoxeny of Abraham'. It is the representation of the well-known scene from *Genesis* in which the Patriarch 'gives hospitality to God' (this is the meaning of the word *theoxenie*), who visited him in the form of three human beings of identical appearance. See the reproduction in the plates.

13. All that follows is according to P. Evdokimov, *The Art of the Icon: A Theology of Beauty*, Redondo Beach, CA, 1990, pp245–257.

rock, and is resolved in the vertical posture of the angel on the left—the Father—where it comes to rest. Besides this circular movement, the icon shows a square table with the eucharistic cup. At the center of the picture is the Tree of Life; its vertical passes through the vertical of the foot of the Cup and the hieroglyph of the earth: the small rectangle painted on the outer face of the table; to which is added the vertical of the Temple situated above the angel on the left. All this symbolism expresses the Fall (the small rectangle 'fallen' to the foot of the Tree of Life), the aspiration of the Earth towards heaven (the verticals), the redemption, the work of the Son (in the middle), realized through the Cup, the central position of which places it in relation to the Heart of God and Creation, and which feeds the Tree of Life bearing the fruits of eternal life, and finally, the reintegration of all things in God figured by the table which is inscribed within the Trinitarian Circle. Notice how the hands of the angels converge towards the sign of the earth; the world, in fact, is separated from God, as being of a different nature, yet is included in the sacred circle of the 'communion of the Father'; it follows the circular movement which is resolved for the world, in the palace temple, figure of the Church. The temple rests in the immobility of the repose of the 'Great Sabbath', the term of the Trinitarian movement. The cycle of the cosmic mystery is closed; this is the eschatological vision of the New Jerusalem, but through the mediation of the eucharistic sacrifice.